Excellent Investing

Mark Simpson

While the principles contained in this manuscript are based on empirical research and applied logic, there is no guarantee that the methods described will be profitable, owing to the inherent risk of stock market investments. This book should not be considered financial advice. Readers are specifically advised to seek professional financial advice if they are unsure about the application of any of the principles described. Neither the publisher nor the author assumes liability for any losses that may be sustained by the use of the methods described in this book and any such liability is hereby expressly disclaimed.

Copyright © 2019 Mark Simpson

The moral right of the author has been asserted.

Copyright © 2019 Productivity Partners Limited

All rights reserved.

No part of this publication may be reproduced, stored in a retrieval system, or transmitted in any form or by any means, without the prior permission in writing of the author, nor be otherwise circulated in any form of binding or cover other than that in which it is published and without a similar condition including this condition being imposed on the subsequent purchaser.

ISBN 978-1-07-494479-7

Contents

Preface 1
Introduction 3

Part One Play to Your Strengths 9
1 Competitive Advantage 11
2 Think Small 21
3 Think Long Term 31
4 Think Differently 43
5 Know Yourself 55

Part Two Overcome Your Weaknesses 83
6 Behavioural Biases 85
7 Overcoming Overconfidence 95
8 Overcoming Loss Aversion 121
9 Overcoming Optimism Bias 129
10 Overcoming Commitment Bias 165

Part Three An Optimal Portfolio 175
11 Creating an Optimal Portfolio 177
12 Maintaining an Optimal Portfolio 207
Conclusion 219

Appendix A	The Kelly Formula	223
Appendix B	Bayes Formula	227
Notes and References		229

Excellent Investing

How to Build a Winning Portfolio

Preface

This book is written for an investor who is looking to elevate their investment performance to the next level. Part One describes the unique advantages that individual investors have in the stock market. Parts Two and Three show how to avoid preventable investment errors and build an optimal portfolio, and will be useful for all types of investors.

There are other books written on how to avoid investment mistakes but too often they miss the mark. Some books promise much but turn out to be merely long-winded arguments for passive investing. While there is nothing wrong with passive investing, recommending it to an investor who prefers to choose their own investments is a bit like recommending a break-up to a friend who asks for advice on improving their romantic relationship. It isn't the type of advice they asked for and will be ignored, no matter how well-intentioned it is. Other books go into great detail on all the mistakes that investors can make but provide little practical advice on how to avoid them, leaving the investor more knowledgeable but ultimately in the same position as before.

In contrast, this book is a practical guide for committed stock-pickers; it will enable you to maximise the return from your investing skill, avoid common investment mistakes and build a winning portfolio.

Introduction

An increasing number of people are choosing their own stock market investments. When interest on savings is so low, final salary pensions are disappearing and trust in the financial sector is weak, the drive to go your own way has never been stronger. For individual investors, the investing landscape has never looked so good either. Information that once cost thousands of pounds a year to access is now readily available for free or little cost. Technology has given timely access to company information and connection to communities of knowledgeable like-minded individuals. The cost of buying and selling shares is now a low, fixed-fee for almost all investors. Some brokers are even offering commission-free trading.

Despite this revolution, the majority of smaller investors still significantly underperform the market. Somehow the greater availability of information and lower costs hasn't resulted in better investment performance. In a 2011 study of over 65,000 investment accounts, Brad Barber and Terrance Odean showed that the average individual investor underperformed the market by 3.7% a year.[1] Part of the underperformance was caused by excessive trading: on average, the accounts that traded the most had the lowest returns. The majority of under-performance, however, was simply due to poor decision-making: the stocks that the average individual investor sold in any given year outperformed the stocks that they bought in that year.

Putting this in monetary terms illustrates the dramatic impact of this shortfall. US equities have averaged 6.5% real annual compound return from 1900-2017.[2] So underperforming the market by 3.7% a year is the difference between £10,000 becoming £229k or £661k, in real terms, over a 30-year investment period. Individual investors who simply avoided poor investment decisions retired with *three times* the income.

So why has this favourable landscape not led to better individual investor performance? And what can you do differently to make sure your investment performance is a positive outlier amongst investors?

Firstly, you can choose to invest only where you have an edge. Warren Buffett makes the analogy of a game of poker:

> Indeed, if you aren't certain that you understand and can value your business far better than Mr. Market, you don't belong in the game. As they say in poker, "If you've been in the game 30 minutes and you don't know who the patsy is, you're the patsy".[3]

Markets are competitive. The average investor must earn the market return minus costs; this is a mathematical certainty. Which means that for an investor to outperform the average, someone else must underperform. Every time you are buying, someone else is selling. It is not enough to know a lot about a company you invest in, you have to know more than the investor who is taking the other side of your trade. In Part One, 'Play to Your Strengths', I explain why having a competitive advantage is so important, what competitive advantages you have, and ways to exploit them. I also describe how successful investors develop their own unique strategy that plays to the strengths of their personality.

Secondly, you need to find a way to overcome what are known as *behavioural biases*: ways in which our decision-making process ends up being consistently flawed. Over the years, psychologists and behavioural economists have done a comprehensive job defining and categorising behavioural biases. Unfortunately, our increased knowledge of these biases doesn't seem to change our behaviour and correct our decision-making. Ironically, one of these is called the *blind spot bias*, where we are unable to recognise our own biases and take appropriate action to modify our behaviour. Daniel Kahneman is one of the psychologists who pioneered this scientific field, and despite winning the Nobel Prize in Economic Sciences for his ground-breaking research and writing a comprehensive book on the subject, Kahneman struggles to consistently correct his decision-making, saying 'I'm better at detecting other people's mistakes than my own.'[4] It seems we can read all about behavioural biases, understand them in great detail, but it does little to stop us falling for them.

Are we forever doomed to failure by our biases?

I don't think so. Although you may fail to recognise the effect of a behavioural bias when you make a specific decision, the consistent nature of behavioural biases means that it is possible to identify in advance where you may be prone to error, enabling you to put in place strategies to mitigate the impact of those biases. In Part Two, 'Overcome Your Weaknesses', I describe not just the major behavioural biases which may lead you to make poor decisions, but ways of reducing the impact of these by developing a specific set of rules to apply to your portfolio.

A significant amount of investment writing is dedicated to stock selection. While good stock-picking is vital to those who seek to outperform the market, it is only part of the story. Of equal importance to your long-term wealth is the ability to build your stock picks into a coherent portfolio, yet this part of the investment process often receives far less attention than it deserves, leaving the average investor under-skilled in this area. In Part Three, 'An Optimal Portfolio', I aim to close that gap: explaining how to create and maintain an optimal portfolio based on sound logical principles.

By playing to your strengths, overcoming your weaknesses and building an optimal portfolio, you will not only avoid the underperformance that haunts many individual investors but lay the foundation for the kind of outperformance that will provide a secure financial future for you and your family.

As the examples of this book will show, professional investors are also prone to making preventable investment errors and ending up with suboptimal portfolios. So, while the application may look different in a professional context, the principles of Parts Two and Three apply equally to the professional investor.

Developing these ideas has been a personal journey of over 15 years of investing in individual stocks. My journey started, as many did, with an *optimistic bias*: my first purchase in 2003 was a gold explorer with "assets" in some far-flung land and no finance to produce any gold. It continued with *overconfidence*: entering the great financial crisis in 2008 over-exposed to leveraged equities. *Loss aversion* has caused me to hang on to stocks in companies that had poor prospects simply because I would be selling at a loss. *Anchoring* has seen me sell at the first bounce back to my buy-price and miss out on gains. While I will doubtless continue to make mistakes, applying these principles to my portfolio has allowed me to generate consistent market-beating returns over the last decade. They have the potential to do the same for you.

Part One

Play to Your Strengths

1
Competitive Advantage

Competitive advantage is one of the most important concepts for investing: it means being able to do something valuable that others can't or find difficult to do. A company with a competitive advantage will often earn high returns on the capital invested in the business: it does what others can't, which allows it to charge higher prices or have lower costs for its products or services.

Conversely, a company without a competitive advantage will not earn a return above its cost of capital over the long term. It will have prices dictated to it by customers, who will have many options for its goods or services.

Even if a company has a competitive advantage today, those high profit margins will attract competitors who will try to erode that competitive advantage over time. This can be seen in the corporate measures that indicate the presence of a competitive advantage, such as return on invested capital. These measures tend to mean-revert over time.[1] Companies that currently generate high returns on capital tend, on average, to see it decrease over time as competitors seek to share in those supra-normal profits. Companies that currently generate a poor return on their invested capital tend to see it increase over time. They are pushed by their owners to improve their efficiency, reduce their working capital, invest in better products, or shut down unprofitable business lines.

It is because of this competitive pressure that value stocks have beaten growth stocks over the long term.[2] Value stocks are usually defined as those that are lowly rated using investment metrics such as price-to-book or price-to-earnings. This reflects the market's concerns about the near-term earnings potential of such stocks. Over periods of less than a year, the group of value stocks shows much lower earnings growth than the general market. After 3-4 years, though, such value stocks have returned, on average, to the earnings growth rate of the general market.[3] Conversely, growth stocks - those that are highly-rated on investment metrics - show much better near-term prospects, yet over several years their growth rates mostly settle back down to market averages.

The reason value stocks have historically generated a higher return than growth stocks is that investors underestimate this process of mean reversion: they think that the near-term company prospects also define the long-term trajectory of earnings. On average, the market overestimates, and therefore overpays for, the long-term growth rate of growth stocks, and underestimates, and underpays for that of value stocks. Investors who can systematically take advantage of these mispricings, caused by competitive pressures, may earn an excess return.

Despite operating in competitive markets, not every company sees its high return on capital revert to the mean. Those that can resist the mean reversion are said to possess a *sustainable* competitive advantage. That is, a competitive advantage that cannot be attacked by competitors or it would be very difficult to do so. Examples of sustainable competitive advantages for companies include brands, network effects, or legal monopolies such as patent protection. These act like a *moat* preventing the company from being attacked by competitive forces. Successfully identifying those companies that possess a sustainable competitive advantage and have a large potential market can often generate very high returns for investors.

Warren Buffett started as a value investor, becoming a multi-millionaire by focussing on companies whose poor business performance would turnaround. He became a multi-*billionaire* due to his ability to identify quality companies with a wide competitive moat and a market to grow in:

> The key to investing is not assessing how much an industry is going to affect society, or how much it will grow, but rather determining the competitive advantage of any given company and, above all, the durability of that advantage. The products or services that have wide, sustainable moats around them are the ones that deliver rewards to investors.[4]
>
> Warren Buffett

Although it is widely understood that being able to analyse the competitive advantage of companies is a vital part of success for a stock-picker, many investors forget to apply the same principles of competitive advantage to their own investment practice. Like companies without a competitive advantage, if you are a good analyst but don't have any competitive advantage in investing then you will earn the market return minus your costs. If you are an active investor these costs are likely to be large enough for you to underperform the market. If you are a bad analyst or poor decision-maker you will significantly underperform the market.

The problem is that the things we think are competitive advantages are often not so. We tend to think of our competitive advantage as being good or experienced at something. Having a competitive advantage, however, is not about just about being good at something but good at things that other people are not good at. You don't have to be just good but better than everyone else. If your skills or experience can be replicated or bought-in, that is not a sustainable competitive advantage. To understand this further it is helpful to think through some of the things that *cannot* be sustainable competitive advantages for individual investors and why this is the case:

Intelligence

You may be clever. Most investors I know are. You are unlikely to be the most intelligent person to trade stocks, though. If your strategy requires you to know a large company (even the one you work for) better than a full-time analyst with a PhD and access to the management you are likely to lose. The largest FTSE100 or S&P500 companies are each covered by more than 20 analysts.[5] Their job is to know as much as they can about a company and communicate key investment information to paying clients as effectively as possible. Professional analysts are often given exclusive access to the management of the companies they cover. As the 21st analyst, with limited access to the management, you are highly unlikely to find out information that has a significant impact on the investment case of these large companies, whatever your IQ.

You should be equally wary of relying too much on your specific expertise of an industry sector. While your specialist knowledge *may* form a competitive advantage, large investors often pay for teams of consultants to analyse specific industry trends. Use of *knowledge networks* is becoming increasingly common by hedge funds too: where true experts in their field make themselves available to provide their expert knowledge to investors for a fee. If you are a genuine expert, this can provide a source of investment edge, but it may be naïve to think this cannot be replicated by others.

Speed

However quick a decision-maker you are, you will never compete with a high-frequency trader. In this realm, microseconds are becoming the norm for news reaction. Machine-readable news aggregation is becoming the way that economic news, such as interest rate changes or non-farm payroll data, is integrated into pricing. Hedge funds are purchasing ever-more detailed and timely data sets such as weekly credit card data to analyse spending trends. They are building *Artificial Intelligence* systems to rapidly analyse increasingly complex data-sets. Very few professional funds can afford to compete in this space and the incremental returns to speed have probably already reached a plateau. If you are not already one of these few, you are unlikely to become one of them. They possess the moat, not you.

Work Ethic

If investment returns were proportional to the hours put in then you are always onto a loser. No matter how many hours a week you personally devote to the pursuit, a professional investment firm can simply hire more analysts to out-work you.

Gut Feel

The problem with basing an investment strategy on your feel for the markets is that it is very difficult to get effective feedback on how good your intuition really is. We all suffer from a form of *attribution bias*: where we remember our successful investments and forget the losing ones (or blame them on some external factor). Even if you keep detailed performance records of your investments, it takes a lot of data to be able to show conclusively that your gut feel adds any value.

As an example of why your gut feel probably isn't a competitive advantage, consider the *Value Line Investment Survey*, one of the most highly regarded and widely used independent global investment research resources. In 2004 T*he Wall Street Journal* ran an article describing how, despite the *Value Line Investment Survey* having a great track record of picking winners, the fund set up to follow the recommendations had massively underperformed.[6] The reason, it seems, was that the managers of the fund overruled the survey picks too often, to the detriment of their investment returns.

This is a common investment theme. When Joel Greenblatt's fund became too large to exploit special situations investing (which I cover in Chapter 4, 'Think Differently'), he transitioned to investing based on what he called 'The Magic Formula' which ranked companies on a combination of cheapness (Earnings Yield) and quality (a form of Return on Capital).[7] Greenblatt found that a portfolio of stocks that were rated highly on this ranked combination outperformed the market.

(Although subsequent studies of the Magic Formula by Wes Gray and Toby Carlisle showed that its outperformance could be entirely explained by the cheapness factor not the quality factor.[8]) Greenblatt provided investors with two options: either he would invest for them in a basket of all Magic Formula stocks, or he would provide them with a list of stocks that are rated highly on the Magic Formula and let them choose which to invest in. Buying the whole basket of stocks turned out to be a much better strategy.[9] When individuals chose their own selection of Magic Formula stocks, these portfolios underperformed the whole group by a massive 25% over the two-year period 2009-2011. Again, when people overrode a successful rules-based strategy, their judgement *detracted* from the results.

Even if you are one of the rare few whose intuitive judgement adds value, the market is a complex adaptive system that is continually changing. There is no guarantee that your gut feel will work for ever. You can lose a lot of money until you realise that things have changed.

Although it is unlikely that you will be a successful investor unless you are clever, hardworking and able to make quick decisions based on your accumulated experience, these alone won't bring you success because these are things that anyone who is sufficiently committed can develop. What you need is *edge*: skills or knowledge that not everyone can possess or exploit.

If you know you don't have an edge then one answer is simply don't try to beat the market. Investing is one of the unique pursuits where being average is easily achievable and perfectly adequate. Regularly contributing to a low-cost index tracker will easily beat the vast majority of active managers after costs. Compounding your returns at the rate that a global equity portfolio has historically delivered will generate significant wealth over time. While there is no guarantee that these rates of return will continue going forward, long-term equity returns will likely be higher than other asset classes in all but the most pessimistic of futures. So, for those who don't want to spend the time required, don't enjoy the process of investing, or don't have the temperament to be an individual investor, passive equity investing is a very credible alternative. If you go this route there will still be challenges, primarily avoiding the temptation to try to time the market, but the outcome is still likely to be highly rewarding.

Managed funds are another way of gaining exposure to markets or sectors where you know that you do not have a competitive advantage. The same requirement to assess competitive advantage also applies to the managed funds you buy though. If you want to generate higher returns through anything other than chance, you have to be sure that the *fund manager* has a sustainable competitive advantage. Given the higher fee levels you will pay to invest in a managed fund, and the structural disadvantages fund managers have, (some of which are covered in the next few chapters), you should have a high threshold for identifying sustainable competitive advantage to prefer a fund versus cheaper passive equity options.

While it may be sobering to realise that some of the things that you thought were competitive advantages are not so, there is some good news: as an individual investor, you have unique advantages that you may not have realised before. There are two areas that individual investors can focus on that are often impossible for the professional investor. The first is investing in smaller companies. The second is thinking longer term than the average market participant. I will explore why these are sustainable competitive advantages in the next two chapters.

In addition to these, there is a competitive advantage that all investors can possess, and that is to focus on what are typically called *special situations*. In his original fund, Joel Greenblatt generated 45% compound annual return for 19 years concentrating on situations where other investors were likely to be selling stocks for reasons unrelated to the true underlying value of the business.[10]

While thinking *small*, *long term* or *differently* is important for everyone who wants to be an excellent individual investor, the implementation of these principles can look very different. We each have unique personalities, strengths and weaknesses that will affect how we process and respond to the emotions caused by gaining and losing money. Since all successful investing requires persistence, it is important to find an investment strategy that matches your personal make-up. You are much more likely to stick with an investment strategy if it has a history of long-term outperformance and fits your personality. So, in the last chapter of Part One, I look at some common successful investment styles and the psychology, strengths and challenges that are associated with these.

2
Think Small

For an investment to have any impact on the performance of a fund, a fund manager must have enough of their fund invested in any given position. The exact amount will vary by fund type, but typically this will be around 1% of assets under management. The average UK investment fund is now around £500m. Which means that the average fund must be able to invest a minimum of £5m in a company's stock for it to have any impact on their investment performance.[1] If the market capitalisation of the company is low, say £30m, the fund would struggle to buy the 17% of the equity that £5m would represent. Liquidity constraints and investment rules mean that most funds can't invest a meaningful amount in such small companies. There are approximately 500 UK-listed stocks with a market capitalisation currently less than £30m which are therefore unlikely to be considered for investment by the average UK fund.[2]

In the US the scale is even larger. Russell Kinnel, the editor of Morningstar's Fund investor newsletter, found that the median size at which small cap funds closed themselves to receiving additional capital was $800m.[3] (Funds typically close themselves to new capital at the point that they feel that their size would hamper them from making profitable investments.) The mean US mutual fund size in 2017 was $2.35bn.[4] With this sort of scale, you are unlikely to see even small cap funds investing in companies with a market capitalisation of less than $100m.

Warren Buffett summarised the problem that scale causes for fund managers in the letter he wrote to investors in his Buffett Partnership in 1969 describing why he was closing the partnership:

> ...our $100m of assets further eliminates a large portion of this seemingly barren investment world, since commitments of less than about $3 million cannot have a real impact on our overall performance, and this virtually rules out companies with less than $100 million of common stock at market value.[5]

Due to his investment success, Buffett had seen his assets under management grow to around $100m (almost $700m in 2019 money). This effectively restricted his investments to companies with a market capitalisation of $100m or more. It didn't matter how good the opportunity was, if he couldn't get enough stock to have a meaningful impact on his performance, it simply wasn't worth his time to research and invest.

This problem is probably worse for funds today. The cost of administering a fund in the current regulatory environment is such that active funds with assets under management of less than £100m are unlikely to be viable businesses in the long term. For example, Lars Kroijer describes the problem of launching a fund with small assets under management in his book *Money Mavericks: Confessions of a Hedge Fund Manager*:[6]

> Since many of the charges such as legal set-up, listing fees, administrative fees, clearing fees etc. are fairly fixed, the investors in a small fund take a larger part of the financial burden than if they had been invested in a larger fund....If an investor lost 3-4 per cent per year in expenses by investing with Holte Capital [Kroijer's fund] relative to investing in a larger fund that made our fund raising argument to investors harder, and meant that even with the cash flows from fees with around $14 million in assets under management we would fail to break even.

Because scale is required to run a profitable fund management business, funds won't invest in the smallest of companies no matter how compelling the investment case. There is, therefore, a lack of competition in this space. The sellers when you are buying or buyers when you are selling will be other individual investors such as yourself. This doesn't guarantee that they are uninformed, of course, but it does mean that they are unlikely to have had preferential access to management. They are also more likely to be selling for personal reasons that are not company specific, such as buying a house or getting divorced. In addition, as the Barber and Odean study showed, the average individual investor is particularly prone to poor decision-making.

There are *micro cap funds* which do aim to invest in very small companies but, in order to deploy their assets under management, they have to hold hundreds of companies that meet superficial investment criteria. They will have a simple investment process rather than doing exhaustive research on each investee company. In this case, such funds are probably no more informed than the average individual investor. For example, I have known micro-cap funds to hold obvious frauds because their investment process was too simple to identify the details that would have warned them of this. Despite these setbacks, these funds often still perform well because the number of stocks they hold means that a total loss on a single stock has little impact on their overall results. In reality, these types of funds are a lot closer to small cap trackers than their managers would have you believe.

Funds that invest in smaller companies, run a concentrated portfolio and do detailed research are rare. When they do exist, they will have constraints on the capital they can manage. They are unlikely to employ many analysts since the fees they charge on a small amount of assets under management will not pay many salaries. These analysts will restrict themselves to small areas of the market where they are especially knowledgeable, and there are very few concentrated micro-cap funds in the market. In many ways, these funds can be thought of as sophisticated individual investors. Their activities are worth following but, given their limited size and number, they are unlikely to have any significant impact on the efficiency of the overall market for smaller companies.

Research into smaller companies is far more likely to pay simply because the competition at this end of the market is less fierce. When you buy a stock, the person selling is much more likely to be an individual investor and, as discussed in the 'Introduction', they tend to make poor decisions and underperform the market, on average. In contrast, market pricing for large companies may be getting more efficient. Larry Swedroe found that 20 years ago, 20% of managers generated alpha (excess return versus a benchmark), whereas today that figure is closer to 2%.[7]

There is also an added element that works in favour of the small company investor: if you are good at picking successful undervalued small companies, they will become larger over time as the valuation gap to fair-value closes. If they grow larger, they will become increasingly liquid and therefore meet the criteria for investment by the bigger investment funds. This attracts investment capital and can become a virtuous circle of increasing investment performance leading to a higher market capitalisation, leading to greater institutional fund-flows, leading to greater investment performance for holders who got in early.

The Impact of MiFID II

One of the recent market developments in the EU, including the UK, has been the introduction of a new legislative framework called MiFID II.[8] This has had two impacts on investors in smaller companies. Firstly, it has meant a greater restriction on broker research being made available to individual investors. Secondly, it made doing research a far less profitable venture for investment banks. They must now charge for research separately and can no longer offer it as an incentive for trading commission. This means that the research departments of investment banks have to make money as stand-alone businesses and increasingly the business case for covering smaller companies is not good. When it becomes unprofitable for these brokers to cover the very small companies, they stop doing so. You may still get the *house broker* (the one paid by the company to represent them) producing a research note for a smaller company. However, it is likely to be the least independent of opinions given the commercial relationship between the company and the broker, and there is still no guarantee that the company can make it available to individual investors. Some smaller companies may not even have a research note from their house broker, leaving no forecasts in the market for their future performance.

While the lack of availability or access to research can be frustrating to smaller investors, the upside is that it makes the market less efficient for smaller companies. This adds another reason why, if you are prepared to do the work to understand a business in detail, you can have a sustainable competitive advantage in this arena.

In addition to the lack of competition, there are two further reasons why investing in smaller companies is a good idea. The first is that smaller companies have generated historically higher returns. The second is that the value premium - the extra return one can get from investing in unloved companies - has tended to be concentrated in smaller companies. These conclusions can be controversial, so I will give a brief summary of the academic research in this area and where I believe the current consensus on these topics lies.

The Small Cap Premium

That investing in smaller companies generates higher returns than investing in larger companies has been known ever since investors started measuring stock market performance. This is known as the *small cap premium*. (Premium, in this case, refers to the additional unexpected return you would *receive* from investing in smaller companies, not the amount you would pay, for example, to buy a premium product.) From 1955-2017 UK micro cap stocks have delivered an 18% compound annual return compared with just 12% for large cap stocks.[9] This isn't surprising since smaller companies have much more room to grow, and one of the biggest drivers of investment return is growth in revenue and earnings. The issue with holding smaller companies is that historically they have also been much more volatile than larger companies. If you held just US small caps for the last century you would have had to stomach at least one occasion where you lost almost 90% of your money and several times where you would have lost at least 50%.[10] The important question is not whether they outperform on an absolute basis but whether they do so on a volatility-adjusted one. Otherwise, investors could just buy the more liquid larger companies and use gearing to get the same or higher returns, with the same volatility. You are only receiving a true premium if you are not paying for it in other ways.

In a historic 1981 research paper, Rolf Banz found that there was a small cap premium that could not be explained by market volatility risk alone. The research faced a certain amount of pushback though, summarised here by Cliff Asness, et al.:

> The size premium has been accused of having a weak historical record, being meager relative to other factors, varying significantly over time, weakening after its discovery, being concentrated among microcap stocks, residing predominantly in January, relying on price-based measures, and being weak internationally.[11]

In his research Asness found, however:

> …that these challenges disappear when controlling for the quality, or its inverse "junk", of a firm. A significant size premium emerges, which is stable through time, robust to specification, not concentrated in microcaps, more consistent

> across seasons, evident for non-price-based measures of size, and these results hold in 30 different industries and 24 international equity markets. The resurrected size effect is on par with anomalies such as value and momentum in terms of economic significance and gives rise to new tests of and challenges for existing asset pricing theories.[12]

It seems that the small cap premium is there if, and only if, you avoid the worst quality stocks.

They define a high-quality company as one that:

> ... is well managed and has strong economic and accounting performance, such as high profitability and stability of earnings, good growth prospects, and low risk.[13]

It seems that, overall, if you avoid the poorest quality stocks, you will do better investing in small companies even before you add stock picking skill and portfolio management into the equation.

I explore some ways one can improve the quality of the companies you hold in Chapter 9, 'Overcoming Optimism Bias'.

The Value Premium

Value investors have an additional reason to focus on small company stocks. In the US, over the 50 years from 1964-2014 large cap value stocks beat large cap growth stocks by 2.8% per year, on average.[14] Over the 50 years, you would have three times the money by investing in large cap value instead of large cap growth stocks. *Small* cap value stocks, however, beat small cap growth stocks by 5.9% per annum over the same period.[15] Over those 50 years, you would have *16 times* more money if you had chosen to invest in small cap value instead of small cap growth stocks. Not only was the value premium (excess return) in small cap stocks larger, it was more consistent and more persistent than in large cap stocks.[16]

In addition to this, in a 2004 research paper, Ludovic Phalippou found that the value premium was not just concentrated in the smallest stocks but those with the least institutional ownership.[17] It seems that institutional investors really do tend to shun small value stocks, and therein lies opportunities for the individual investor.

So, before you decide which companies to buy, if you focus your research on smaller companies (and avoid the worst quality ones) you will be swimming with the flow. If you add high effort and good technique (stock selection), you should be able to swim much faster than even powerful swimmers who have to swim upstream. There are genuine reasons to be concerned with the extra volatility that owning small cap stocks may bring your way, but for the individual investor, and especially the value investor, small is the place to be.

3
Think Long Term

> The single greatest edge an investor can have is a long-term orientation.
>
> Seth Klarman

Although many financial market participants claim to be long-term investors, true long-term thinking is surprisingly rare. The structure of the investment industry prevents this from happening by applying a short-term timeframe on the reporting of investment results. Every fund reports its annual performance, most also report quarterly performance and some even provide monthly updates. The average portfolio manager may seem to have their interest aligned with their investors and be incentivised to generate the highest risk-adjusted returns for them, but in reality, their bonus structure creates a slight but important mismatch of incentives. Most managers are paid bonuses according to the excess returns they generate in any given calendar year, so they mostly focus on generating whatever outperformance they can in the next year. To generate true long-term market-beating returns you have to think differently than the market, be right, and wait for the market to come around to your way of thinking. To think differently is hard, to be right even harder, and the wait for the market to align with your view is unpredictable. This dilemma sees most managers leave behind the search for the highest returns and instead settle for playing a game of guess the next quarter's company results. When everyone plays this game, then stock prices respond to how accurately everyone guessed next quarter's sales and earnings, not to the long-term value creation of the business. Stock market analysts estimate quarterly figures that become a consensus. Portfolio managers take positions based on how their view differs from the consensus. The share price movements reward those who guess the short-term results correctly and reinforce the idea that this is the game one needs to play if one is to get a bonus at the end of the year.

The short-term thinking of investment managers even starts to permeate the listed companies themselves. Company managements see the market reaction to quarterly forecasts and understand that the way to keep their shareholders happy is to always hit their quarterly figures. In a 2005 paper, Graham, Harvey and Rajgopal surveyed companies and found that the majority of managers would not implement a project that would have a positive impact on the net present value of the cash flows of the business if it meant that the required investment would cause them to miss their quarterly earnings consensus.[1] The smoothness of earnings was valued more highly than true value creation.

Warren Buffett identified the impact of this as far back as 1969, describing the reason he was closing the Buffett Partnership Limited as:[2]

> ...a swelling interest in investment performance has created an increasingly short term and (in my opinion) more speculative market.

The second factor that causes fund managers to focus overly on short term performance is *career risk*: the chance that they will lose assets under management or their job if they underperform the market for too long. Famously, fund manager Tony Dye, who had been highly sceptical of the tech stock bubble in the late 1990s and refused to buy into it, got fired just two weeks before the bubble began to burst.[3]

A survey by State Street Global Advisors indicated that 89% of asset allocators would look at changing managers after just two years of underperformance.[4] The message to fund managers is clear: if you want to keep your job, it is more important to avoid underperformance than to outperform.

The film *The Big Short*, based on a Michael Lewis book, gives an excellent account of what happens to fund managers whose positions go against them for extended periods of time.[5] It shows Dr Michael Burry bucking conventional wisdom by buying credit default swaps on subprime mortgage-backed securities. Credit default swaps are similar to an insurance policy that pays out if these securities fail, something that had never happened in the past. To hold these credit default swaps Burry's firm, Scion Capital, had to pay monthly fees (similar to an insurance premium). However, if the bonds failed, as they eventually did, these securities paid out many times the monthly fee. The seed investors in Scion Capital included the great investor Joel Greenblatt. Even someone who is used to thinking differently to the market such as Greenblatt couldn't see the logic of the trade, didn't trust Burry's execution of it, or simply needed the money to meet redemptions in his own fund. Either way, he was unwilling to retain his capital with Burry through to the end of the trade. Greenblatt requested a redemption of his funds and Burry invoked an emergency clause in the fund management agreement to prevent the redemption. These clauses are known as *gating* the fund and are designed to protect other investors in the fund in situations where it would require the fund manager to sell highly illiquid securities in a way which would then negatively impact the value of the holdings of the remaining investors. Since Bury felt that the price he was being offered by his counterparties for his credit default swaps was fundamentally incorrect, he refused to sell out to meet the redemption requests. Gating a fund is an extreme step because the manager is refusing to return their own money to investors. Understandably, taking this action soured Burry's relationship with Greenblatt, which never recovered, despite the subsequent stellar returns Burry posted having been proved right about the collapse of the mortgage-backed securities market in 2008.

I don't think Burry got everything right in this trade. By starting it in 2005 he was too early, and he oversized his position for the amount of capital he had. If he had a smaller position, he would have made less money but would have had a lot less stress, and would have been able to meet any redemption requests from selling other more liquid positions. He also failed to convince his investors of the soundness of his strategy so they were willing to stick with him. Nevertheless, this example highlights the pressures that even excellent well-regarded professional money managers face by going against the crowd for extended periods. Burry considered the episode so depressing he closed his fund to external capital in 2008.[6] When investing superstars such as Burry and Greenblatt cannot overcome the short-term thinking of their investors, you can guarantee it affects the behaviour of almost all professional fund managers.

The good news is that if you are only managing your own money you have no-one who can fire you if you underperform the market for significant periods. You don't have to report your performance monthly, quarterly, or yearly, and you don't have to justify it anyone else unless you choose to. Your success will be measured against your own personal financial goals. You are free to invest with a longer-term horizon and this gives you a very real advantage over professional fund managers. Being able to invest for the long term, when most market participants can't, therefore constitutes a sustainable competitive advantage for the individual investor.

Personal Example – Encore Oil

The oil exploration sector provides a useful example for examining the short-term nature of financial markets. Oil explorers own licenses to extract oil and gas assets from specific geographic areas. Governments issue the licenses in return for payments, or commitments to spend certain amounts of money in exploring these areas.

The first step in oil exploration is to shoot seismic surveys over the license to identify potential areas, known as prospects, where oil or gas may be found. Seismic surveys involve making loud sounds over a wide area and then recording the sound waves as they return to a receiver. Different rock formations reflect and refract the sound waves in different ways; hence the type of signal received will vary depending on the subsurface geology. Complex signal processing can turn the recorded sound waves into an estimate of the sub-surface geology. Typically, seismic surveys are shot over the whole of the area that is licensed to an exploration company, particularly for sub-sea exploration since a surface boat can easily access the whole area of interest.

Without drilling, no-one can know how accurate the picture is that the seismic survey has created, or if these prospects contain oil. It is, however, possible to estimate the size range of the potential reservoir from the seismic data and the probability that it might contain oil from data on similar past drilling campaigns. If you then combine these with probability estimates about the economic outcomes, such as the chance of the prospect being commercially viable and the net present value of a recoverable barrel of oil, then you arrive at an estimate of the value of the prospect today. This is known as the Risked Net Asset Value (NAV) and is the mid-case for what the oil field is worth today, risked by the (at this stage very small) chances of it actually being a commercial find.

Although any one oil well could be a success or failure, if the estimates that go into the calculation of Risked NAV are good, then in a portfolio of many assets, the results should converge to the Risked NAV, with the drilling of many wells. Buying a sufficiently diversified selection of oil companies, at a significant discount to a conservative estimate of Risked NAV, is likely to yield positive investment results.

So why does a company often trade at a significant discount to Risked NAV?

Well, it may be because the market doubts the estimates that go into these calculations. It is right to be wary of promotional managements of small cap oil exploration companies that don't (and probably never will) have the money to drill any wells or develop the oil fields. However, even well-financed, conservatively-run oil companies can often trade at a significant discount, primarily because oil exploration is a long process. The wells that determine whether the oil is actually there are often drilled far in the future and will occur at indeterminate times. If a company doesn't have funding for future drilling, or there are other issues, the market may be right to be sceptical. However, often the market places no value on potential accumulations of oil simply because the drilling is planned far in the future. Indeed, analysts who cover oil companies often calculate their estimates of a company's Risked-NAV based only on firm wells planned in the next year because the funds that pay for research often only have a one-year time horizon in which they need to see results for investors. Any wells that are more than one year in the future, even fully funded ones, can be attributed zero or negligible value by the market.

A company called Encore Oil found itself in this situation back in 2010. A failed gas storage project, combined with a drop in the oil price, meant that confidence in the company was really low. So low, in fact, that the company traded below its net cash. The market placed no value on any of the company's potential oil assets, despite it having two wells planned in about 18 months' time that were to be entirely funded by their partners.

When those wells and subsequent follow-up wells were completed, the company had found the *Catcher* oil field: the largest oil discovery in the North Sea since the *Buzzard* field in 2000. Those of us who picked up a holding in the company below net cash did very well, with the share price delivering at least a ten-fold increase over the next couple of years.

Not every investment outcome will be as fortuitous as this but the principle is universal: look for companies where the market is placing no value on potentially valuable assets simply because their likely realisation is beyond professional investors' usual reporting timeframe.

Sometimes you don't even need drilling success to see returns from this strategy. As potential value-realisation events get closer, and into the typical one-year horizon, the market may start to recognise the value of the prospects simply due to the proximity of drilling. For those willing to do the detailed work analysing prospects, oil explorers are a good place to find this sort of mispricing, but it occurs in many other market segments too. Think long term and reap the rewards.

Defensive and Income Strategies

The success of defensive strategies is largely down to their long-term focus. Defensive stocks are those whose business has little correlation to the current economic climate, such as cinemas, or manufacturers of household goods. These businesses can appear uninspiring to investors: they rarely generate high returns in one year and will typically underperform the general market in bullish times. This makes them unappealing to those whose bonus or career is dependent on yearly market-beating returns. Those who can take a longer-term view, however, often generate excess returns by owning such stocks (assuming they are able to choose businesses that have good economics despite their boring appearance). One caution with this strategy, however, is that these types of companies may not always be undervalued. Although their appeal is limited to more aggressive funds, as of writing, the record low-interest environment means that such defensive stocks have become more appealing to conservative investors, who may have typically bought bonds in the past. Given their bond-like appearance to some investors, defensive stocks may now be overvalued and face headwinds when interest rates rise.

Similarly, buying large, securely-financed, dividend-paying stocks on high yields has historically generated a slight outperformance compared to owning an index fund. Companies usually end up with a high dividend yield because their short-term growth prospects are weak, or they are suffering from poor sentiment due to ongoing issues with the economics of their business. The market often over-reacts to such problems though, and those who can take a long-term view often see these resolved and corporate performance mean revert. The returns from thinking long term are enhanced by the regular payments of dividends received while investors wait for the corporate performance to recover and be reflected in the share price.

Although not a terrible idea, investing in companies purely based on their dividend yield is unlikely to be an optimal strategy for most investors: historically, it has been the weakest of the *value factors* that have been shown to generate outperformance.[7] If your strategy involves buying unloved stocks and holding for as long as it takes for them to become loved (or at least less hated), it is likely that you will generate higher returns using one of the other *value* metrics, such as high earnings yield or shareholder yield (dividends plus buybacks minus equity issuance, all divided by share price). Income investing has a superficial attraction to many investors who rely on their investments for their everyday living expenses; there is something comforting about automatically receiving a steady stream of dividends rather than having to make active selling decisions to raise cash. In investing, comfort often comes at the cost of performance, though, particularly to those in countries where income is taxed at a higher rate than capital gains. Some people may accept lower returns from an income strategy versus an earnings-based value strategy because they find it easier to stick to over the long term, but they should do so conscious of the trade-off they are making, including the tax implications they face.

Another popular income-based strategy is *dividend growth investing*. The theory is that if you buy stocks where the dividend is increasing then the share price will follow over time. This appears to be a logical way to invest, but it simply isn't backed up by the data. Historically, dividend growth investing has generated *lower* returns than a strategy of investing in the highest yielding stocks, which in turn has performed worse than other forms of value investing.[8] I see little reason why anyone would want to engage in dividend growth investing given that superior returns are available from simpler income strategies.

One way that dividend payments may help you generate significant outperformance is when they act as a strong signal of management intentions. If a company is going through a difficult trading period but a trustworthy management team still increases the dividend payment, it is a clear signal that the management believes that the issue is being dealt with effectively. Conversely, if a company presents a confident outlook but holds its dividend payout, they may be expecting more cautious trading conditions ahead.

Thinking long term isn't merely about being able to hold stocks for an extended period, although that will undoubtedly be required sometimes. It is about identifying where short-term concerns and structural market features, such as fund manager remuneration, create myopia in the majority of market participants and taking advantage of that; looking through short-term missteps to see the long-term value of businesses.

Long-Term Professional Investors

Although I describe long-term thinking as a moat of the individual investor, there is one group of professional investors who can join you on the long-term investing train: those who have permanent capital, such as managers of closed-end funds. Investors in closed-end funds have no right of redemption; they can sell the shares of the fund in the market but they cannot access the capital directly.

It is no coincidence that Berkshire Hathaway, the investment vehicle that has made Warren Buffett one of the world's richest men, has permanent capital. (It also has non-recourse leverage. Owning an insurer and investing the insurance float adds additional return without giving up its permanent capital.) Even this fund structure doesn't completely remove the incentive for portfolio managers to think short term; managers may still focus on short-term results in order to generate personal bonuses, but by having permanent capital such fund managers are immune to the problem of being fired for underperformance. (Technically, fund managers are employees or contractors and can be fired by the trustee, but this very rarely happens. Presumably, because the fund managers tend to be substantial shareholders themselves, and investors usually "buy into" the investment philosophy and reputation of the fund manager, not the specific fund vehicle.) The well-run permanent capital funds can focus on making decisions that generate the highest long-term risk-adjusted returns for investors. By thinking long term, you can too.

4
Think Differently

The ability to generate outperformance by *thinking differently* is a feature of any competitive market where structural inefficiencies exist. The driver is often the *price-insensitive* selling of assets for reasons other than changes in valuation. The concept is illustrated nicely by an example from a market that investors may be less familiar with: the corporate bond market.

Corporate bonds are commonly given credit ratings by ratings agencies. These ratings are based on each agency's view of the likelihood of the company defaulting on its debt. The ratings range from the most creditworthy, AAA, down to the most speculative, CCC, with several categories in between. The market typically uses these ratings to price the bonds. Investors who are bearing more credit risk, by buying bonds with a greater chance that the principle will not be repaid, will want a higher yield to compensate them for bearing this risk.

The overall return to investors in a portfolio of bonds will be the total of the principal returned on bonds that don't default, plus the interest paid over time, minus the loss on any bonds that have defaulted. Two terms are commonly used to categorise these bond ratings: *Investment Grade*, and *High Yield (*or *Junk* bonds as they are colloquially called).

So which category do you think generates the highest average return to investors?

It may surprise you to learn that, despite a much larger number of defaults occurring, it is the Junk bonds that generate the highest risk-adjusted returns over the long term. Not all Junk bonds outperform though; the lowest rated, CCC, have underperformed treasuries (very safe short-term government debt) since 1984.[1]

Why does this happen?

In his book *Expected Returns*, Antti Ilmanen explains that:[2]

> The BB-rated sector, just below the IG [Investment Grade] threshold, provides the best long-run performance of any bond category. This relative success likely reflects partial market segmentation caused by the constraints under which many portfolio managers operate. Fallen angels ("orphan" bonds downgraded from IG to HY [High Yield], which IG portfolio managers are forced to sell) appear to outperform bonds originally issued as HY.

Let's go through what appears to be happening in a bit more detail. In an attempt to reassure investors, many bond funds have a rule in their investment charter that restricts them to holding only the safest of issues: Investment Grade bonds. When a bond is downgraded by a ratings agency below Investment Grade, the funds are forced to sell these bonds. It doesn't matter if the portfolio manager believes that the bond is unlikely to default, or that the low price more than compensates for the increased risk, their investment rules say they must sell. Since

Investment Grade bond funds dominate the market, the number of forced sellers can easily exceed the number of willing buyers. In these market conditions, those who buy the recently downgraded bonds from forced sellers tend to get a relative bargain. This leads to the highest rated Junk bonds, those most likely to contain bonds recently downgraded from Investment Grade, having the highest *Information Ratio* (a measure of excess return after adjusting for volatility).

This example perfectly illustrates the principle of *think differently*. It isn't about always taking the opposite view to everyone else, (such as buying the lowest-rated bonds), betting against the market at all times is unlikely to be a winning strategy since it often prices securities quite efficiently. Instead, the key is to identify those areas where other market participants are likely to be selling for reasons that are unrelated to the valuation of the asset. This is where market inefficiency, and therefore great investment returns, are often found.

Since individual investors are unlikely to be building portfolios of recently downgraded corporate bonds, in the rest of this chapter I will introduce some ideas for where these types of special situations may be found in the equity markets, starting with probably the best known – spin-offs.

Spin-offs

Joel Greenblatt's phenomenal investment returns came from recognising that this same dynamic of price-insensitive selling occurs in the equity markets in a series of special situations known as *spin-offs*. A spin-off occurs when a company decides to list a non-core business unit as a separate company on the stock market.

The usual process is that, if you have 1,000 shares of the parent company on the date of the spin-off, you will still own your 1000 shares of the parent company, but will be also allocated 1000 shares of the spin-off non-core business unit as a separate company. If the market has priced the deal efficiently, the value of your shares will be the same, just that the value will be split between two holdings instead of one. However, the market rarely prices these situations well. A study by Penn State, based on 25 years of data, showed that spin-offs outperformed the market by 10% per year, with the majority of the outperformance occurring in the second year after the spin-off date.[3] The reason for this effect is that people often sell their shares in the spin-off for reasons unrelated to the value of the underlying business; because the investment potential of that business unit is unlikely to be the reason they invested in the parent company and the spin-off is an unknown company without detailed historical investment information.

In his book, *You Can Be a Stock Market Genius*, Greenblatt explains factors that may improve the chances that the spin-off company will not be priced correctly.[4] With each of these factors, you can see why they may contribute to an increase of price-insensitive selling:

The spin-off company has unpopular characteristics

If the spin-off company is in an industry that is suffering from poor market sentiment, has low returns on capital, or is highly indebted, then these characteristics will make the company unattractive to its new owners. Not every unpopular spin-off will be a bargain, but there may be signs that some spin-offs are not as bad as they initially appear. For example, if a strong management team decides to go to the spin-off company rather than stay with the parent, this is a sign that they see a bright future for the stand-alone business. It may also reduce the risk of informational asymmetry: where the company management knows something bad about the future of the spin-off company, or its industry, that you don't know.

The spin-off company is much smaller than the parent company.

The spin-off company is more likely to be mispriced than the parent company. If the spin-off company is small, it will form an insignificant part of an investor's portfolio. Investors are more likely to see a small holding in a company they don't know well and sell it, particularly if they view them as something they got for free. Institutional investors may not be able to get the size of holding that they need to invest in the spin-off and sell, even if they view it as an attractive investment. When a parent company is part of an index, the smaller spin-off may not qualify for that index and you may see index funds selling out too.

The spin-off company is in a different business sector to the parent.

Larger investors may own a company due to a positive view on the sector that a company operates in, not the individual company. Being in a different sector, then, will cause the spin-off to be sold. As with index funds, sector funds or ETFs may become forced sellers too.

You wait a period of time before investing.

Greenblatt found that the indiscriminate selling of the spin-off company happened for about six months or more. However, you have to remember that markets are adaptive; they change their behaviour based on past observed behaviour. Which means that if clever special situation investors are looking for these opportunities, they will want to buy earlier than other investors. We may see the period of mispricing shorten, compared with when Greenblatt wrote his book in 1999.

None of these factors guarantees a good investment, though. You will still need to do good fundamental valuation work to be a successful spin-off investor. The more of these factors you see in a spin-off situation, however, the more likely you are to see a good company selling at a fundamentally mispriced level.

While spin-offs are probably still some of the richest veins of outperformance for a special situations investor, there are other well-known cases where investors sell for reasons not related to their assessment of the fundamental value of the company.

Year-End and Tax Year Effects

Artificial deadlines, such as reporting year-ends, may cause stock mispricing. At year-end, investment funds write to their investors to report on their investment strategy and recent performance. They will often list their significant holdings and describe which holdings have contributed to their returns. Most investment funds are structured in a way that incentivises them to maximise their *Assets Under Management,* not necessarily their returns. Which means that how they are perceived by investors matters a lot. Their year-end review is not just a statement of facts but acts as a marketing document too; it helps to re-assure existing investors or potential future clients that the fund manager has a good strategy and is executing it well.

Even if fund managers have performed high-quality analysis, poor recent performance will not help market the fund to investors. If a fund holds a losing stock, they may be tempted to sell it prior to the year-end so they can avoid declaring it as a holding and writing about it in their annual review. If a fund is interested in buying the stock because they believe the market has over-reacted to bad news, it is a lot safer for them to buy it after year-end; this gives more time for a recovery to occur before having to report it to fund investors.

This combination of funds selling out at any price and hesitant buyers can cause further price declines such that the stock trades significantly below fundamental value. That most funds' reporting period ends just after Christmas, when liquidity is reduced by fewer active market participants, means that this effect can be exaggerated further. It pays to keep one eye on the markets during those times for illiquid companies that demonstrate unexpected price weakness on no news. You may be getting a bargain.

Likewise, the artificial deadline of the end of the tax year may cause price-insensitive selling. In many countries the tax year ends on 31 December and will help exaggerate the year-end effects. In the UK the personal tax year ends on 5 April so you may see unusual price movements in the run up to that date. Again, the effect is usually concentrated in stocks that have generated losses for investors in recent periods. However, in this case, it is the desire of individual investors to crystallise losses to offset capital gains that is the reason for the selling rather than the desire to avoid reporting on poor performing stocks.

Liquidity Events

A similar effect can occur when funds become forced sellers for other reasons. Sometimes the parent company of a fund is wound down and a fund is forced to sell all its holdings in the market. Sometimes funds face large redemptions which cause them to sell some of their holdings. These can cause specific stocks to become undervalued.

More general market liquidity events can also occur: where the broad market declines by so much that those who have invested using leverage become forced sellers, which, in turn, causes prices to decline so that more investors become forced sellers and the market spirals downward. This is one of the reasons why markets tend to grind upwards but crash downwards. When these events occur, then many investment opportunities become available, as many stocks are sold way below a conservative estimate of their intrinsic value.

There are some problems with taking advantage of these opportunities though. For example, such large general market declines are quite rare, and you have to leave cash sitting on the sidelines for significant periods to be able to take advantage. Probably the biggest impediment to taking advantage of these, however, is that they happen when the whole financial world looks like it is going down the pan. What started as a liquidity event often starts to look a lot more like a solvency event. It takes a brave person, with a unique mindset, to be buying in size at these times, particularly because the market could easily drop much further from where you purchased. For this reason, it is much easier to look for stock specific overhangs and forced selling than wait for general market liquidity events, no matter how profitable these may be.

Other Special Situations

There are occasional inefficiencies where the market fails to react quickly enough to news.

> ### Personal Example – Pure Wafer
>
> In August 2015 a UK company called Pure Wafer announced that they would return 140-145 pence per share to shareholders following an insurance payout related to a fire in the UK part of their business. The shares opened that day at 145 pence to buy in the market, possibly due to weak market sentiment in the summer of 2015, or maybe because the company had already shown significant gains over the prior months leaving some investors already over-weight. Whatever the reason, given that the company still retained a profitable US trading business, it was highly unlikely that the shares were worth less than the 145 pence purchase price. I used all of the spare cash in my dealing account to purchase shares and even used a small amount of leverage to add to the position. The shares rapidly rose to 165 pence that day as others realised the opportunity and, following the sale of the trading business, the company returned more than 180 pence per share in total to investors. While the size of the return is not significant in absolute terms, those buying the stock at 145 pence were getting a virtually risk-free return of almost 30%. The market rarely offers a free lunch, but when it does you need to stuff yourself.

Although the presence of a cash return equivalent to the current share price is an obvious example of such inefficiency, in general, it is under-reaction to unexpected very positive news flow that may provide these opportunities.

I have also seen share prices fail to react efficiently to events, such as trading without the rights to a dividend or capital return, when the situation is particularly complicated. Normally, on the date that shareholders lose the right to receive a dividend or other payment, the share price would drop by the same amount to reflect the change of ownership of that cash from the company to the individual stockholders directly. If the share price doesn't react on that date, you may be able to sell at a high price *and* receive the dividend, or payment. These inefficiencies are often fleeting. To take advantage you have to be quick to analyse the situation and have confidence in your analysis. Although these types of situation can be highly lucrative, they are very rare and the amount of capital that can be deployed in them will usually be limited. They make a nice bonus if you can spot them but cannot be relied upon as a more extensive investment strategy.

Merger Arbitrage

Merger arbitrage involves assessing the likelihood of announced takeover offers completing in order to react to any perceived market mispricing. Usually this involves buying the takeover candidate at a discount to the offer price and, if the takeover has a stock component, shorting the buyer. If the takeover is successful, the strategy makes money whatever the intervening market movements. This strategy attracts special situation hedge funds because the return it generates is uncorrelated to the general market, and hedge funds can do extensive due diligence on the takeover situations to assess their likelihood to succeed.

Individual investors are unlikely to have a competitive advantage in this area though, and the return profile is distinctly unappealing for the average investor: when things go right you make a small return, but when things go wrong you suffer a significant loss. Such strategies only work when you diversify across many situations and are very good at getting your analysis right. For these reasons, most individual investors are better off avoiding these types of strategies.

In general, the same goes for other types of sophisticated arbitrage strategies. Although delta-hedging (buying convertible bonds and shorting the equity), or corporate structure arbitrage (simultaneously buying and shorting different parts of a company's capital structure), may be lucrative for hedge funds, they are complex, difficult to implement, and risky for the individual investor.

In summary, there are many good special situations that the individual investor with the right mindset can take advantage of. The key to success in this area is finding those places in the market where investors are selling for reasons other than a fundamental assessment of value or may be significantly underreacting to news, and *think differently* to the average market participant.

5
Know Yourself

Whatever investment style you develop, it will likely suffer from long periods of underperformance relative to the general market. If an investment style was easy to implement and successful all the time then everyone would do it, and thus it would stop working. Investment styles that work over the long term are the ones that are hard to implement for psychological reasons.

Value investors go through long periods of underperformance; usually late in the economic cycle, as market participants extrapolate earnings growth of high-growth stocks too far into the future and overpay for them.

Momentum investors suffer very sharp reversals when the strategy abruptly stops working (often early in a market recovery).[1]

Even *quant* funds, which try to identify mispriced securities by using computer models to identify *all* characteristics that have historically outperformed, have had their bad periods.[2] Since most quant funds use the same ideas and research to guide their computer models, their trades can become *crowded*; every quant fund ends up owning a very similar portfolio and often use leverage to generate the level of returns investors require. This means that selling at one fund can trigger selling at another fund and a domino effect occurs, leading to short periods of rapid decline as many funds try to liquidate the same positions.

If you don't think your strategy will ever face these sort of difficulties, consider the results of a cleverly-titled study by Wes Gray: *Even God Would Get Fired as an Active Investor*.[3] Gray examined what would happen if you were omniscient, and knew for sure which the best performing 50 stocks would be in the S&P500 over the following five years, and invested in those. Unsurprising, the long-term returns you would get from investing in this "cheating" look-ahead portfolio, rebalanced regularly, are exceptional: almost 29% compound per annum from 1927-2016. What is surprising is that, despite absolutely knowing that these would be the best stocks to invest in for the next five years, you would still face gut-wrenching draw-downs. There would have been ten occasions when the look-ahead portfolio would have lost 20% or more, including one loss of 75%. If being omniscient doesn't allow you to avoid periods of large draw-down, it is almost certain you will face one at some point in your investing career.

Successful implementation of an investment strategy requires that you are able to stick with your strategy through the inevitable periods of underperformance. Excellent investing, therefore, requires *grit*.

Grit

Psychologist, Angela Duckworth, defines grit as: 'perseverance and passion for long-term goals'.[4] Grit, therefore, has two components: perseverance of effort and the ability to hold interest over time. Although grit is related to *conscientiousness*, which is one of the big five personality traits that most psychologists use to assess personality, it is considered to be distinct from it. (The other big five personality traits are Openness, Extroversion, Agreeableness and Neuroticism.)

Grit is not related to intelligence, and in fact, is a better predictor of success than IQ. Grit is particularly associated with overcoming obstacles and adversity, which is why it is important for successful investors to possess. Financial markets provide constant perceived adversity: they continually provide feedback that compares your performance to that of the general market, other investors, or even just your own recent past. No strategy offers consistently high performance with low drawdowns over long periods. (If someone offers you this they are most likely to be a Bernie Madoff figure and you should run away as fast as you can.) Without grit, these periods of underperformance, which we will all face, are likely to lead to poor decision-making.

Grittier people are more able to focus on long-term goals without needing immediate feedback.[5] They are more able to ignore the perceived adversity when an investment strategy does not show short-term results and stay the course, rather than chopping and changing to whatever seems "hot" at the time. While I don't doubt that some people are able to perceive the way investment trends and money flows will go and exploit these fads, evidence suggests that most investors have very poor market-timing instincts. Grittier people are more able to overcome those wealth-destroying urges.

Grittier people work harder and longer than their less gritty peers.[6] Although work-ethic alone is not sufficient to provide investment success, you are unlikely to generate meaningful outperformance unless you commit significant time to the endeavour, and grit will help you put the hours in.

Like most aspects of personality, our natural level of grittiness is probably set at a relatively young age by our genetics and our environment. Not all is lost, however, if you don't currently have a naturally gritty personality. There is evidence that grit is, at least partially, domain-specific. I.e. we can be gritty in some pursuits but not others.

What makes the difference?

Primarily the level of enjoyment we get from the activity. Find what works, and what you love about investing, and do more of that; by doing this you are more likely to increase your grittiness and hence stay consistent in the face of adversity.

There are some other ways that you can enhance your grittiness too. Develop a *growth mindset*. Carol Dweck coined this term to represent an underlying system of beliefs that one can learn, develop and improve.[7] When you view your investment practice as a journey where you will be constantly learning and developing skills over a lifetime, the setbacks you face will be interpreted as learning opportunities rather than failures.

Try to avoid comparing your performance to others. Although benchmarking your long-term (5-year plus) performance versus a relevant index is a good idea to check that your efforts have added value, continually comparing your short-term performance to other investors is unlikely to help bring you success, or indeed happiness. There is a reason that Warren Buffett talks so much about the importance of your *inner scorecard*. If he had given in to external pressure from others and shifted to invest in tech stocks in 1999, he would have a significantly worse investment performance record. The temptation is to see the short-term success of others as a need to modify your strategy unnecessarily. Follow and learn from the principles shared by great investors but ignore their short-term returns.

The same goes for publicly sharing your short-term results. Knowing that public comparison with short-term benchmarks is the undoing of many professional investors, why do it when you don't have to?

Some people may have reasons for sharing that aren't related to an *external scorecard*, but the desire for the admiration of others is usually present in all of us. The cost of that admiration may well be poor future decision-making. As Rolf Dobelli puts it:

> Whichever way you look at it, the truth is that people desire external gain because it nets them internal gain. The question that suggests itself is obvious: why take the long way round? Just take the direct route.[8]

Be happy that your long-term investment success will provide a secure financial future for you and your family, and leave the investing glory to those who want to risk its potentially damaging sheen.

Investment Styles

Sticking with a successful investment strategy is much easier when it fits your unique personality. The type of investor you are will be determined, to some extent, by both your genetics and your formative life history.[9] Which is unsurprising given that both of these are shown to be strong determiners of personality.[10] In a study using data on Swedish twins, Henrik Cronqvist found that whether an investor favoured growth or value investing was much more correlated in identical twins than non-identical twins (who share less genetic material).[11] Although it is hard to identify the impact of specific life experiences, the same study showed that external factors, such as the rate of economic growth during an investor's lifetime, did impact how likely they were to be value or growth investors; higher rates of economic growth correlated with a higher preference for growth investing.

Probably the most common personality assessment investors are given is one intended to assess their attitude to risk. This is often administered by financial advisors or pension providers to determine the suitability of the products they are selling to investors. If such assessments prevent the unscrupulous from putting old ladies into badly structured high-fee funds they are a good thing, but for most investors there's not much value in these metrics. They tend to be poor at demonstrating the real-life consequences of the decisions that investors make and seem to be set up to protect the advisor not act in the best interest of the investor. An investor with a low risk-tolerance may have to accept higher volatility than they would normally be comfortable with if they need a higher return to meet their retirement needs. Equally, an investor who is already independently wealthy would be foolish to have a significant proportion of their wealth in volatile high-risk funds, even if they were highly risk-tolerant. A good advisor should assess both an investor's attitude towards risk alongside their need to take risk and help them implement the resulting plan. In my experience, without guidance, most people just end up picking the middle risk-rating, mainly because they don't really have any better idea of their risk tolerance even after conducting the assessment.

Risk tends to be domain specific as well; being risk-seeking or risk-averse in one area of life, such as health, doesn't correlate well with other areas of life, such as financial planning.[12] Most financial advisors would consider my investment style to be high-risk since I invest almost exclusively in small cap value stocks. This doesn't mean I take significant risks in other areas of life, though, such as how I drive my car.

Making sure you are comfortable with the risks you are taking with your investments is important, and ensuring they are not creating undue stress is valuable, but most people don't need an arbitrary test to achieve this: you know if you are able to sleep at night.

Johnathan Meyers, a research fellow in investment psychology and behavioural finance at Columbia University, has attempted to categorise investors based on their personality. In his book, *Profits Without Panic: Investment Psychology for Personal Wealth*, he splits investors into six main types: Cautious, Emotional, Technical, Busy, Casual and Informed.

Cautious investors take time to weigh up investments and only act when they are sure they are on to a good thing. They also tend to be loss-averse, which, as I explain in Chapter 8, 'Overcoming Loss Aversion', can cause poor decision-making.

Emotional investors tend to act on a whim. They prefer gut feel to detailed analysis and may fail to seek out all the necessary information to make good decisions. I have already covered why relying too much on gut feel in your investment practice is not a good idea in Chapter 1, 'Competitive Advantage'.

Technical investors like to have large amounts of information to make decisions. They often seek out the best technology, or fastest data sources, in an attempt to generate an investment edge.

Busy investors love the buzz that investment decisions give them. They feel action adds value and tend to be shorter-term holders of investments.

Casual investors tend to set an initial course and then leave their investments to themselves. They are often busy with other things and rely on professional advice to make their decisions.

Informed investors are good at seeking out the information they need and using it to make sound investment decisions. They are good at seeking the opinions of others but are not unduly influenced by them.

While identifying your investor type from Meyers' categories, (his book contains a personality test for this), may help you avoid some areas of weakness, there are a couple of issues with applying this categorisation as an individual investor.

One of them is that investors from several of those categories are unlikely to make good individual stock-pickers. The slow-to-act cautious investor, the emotional investor acting on a whim, or the casual investor who doesn't commit much time to their investments are unlikely to be successful in this field. It might be useful to know if you are one of those types of investors, and therefore should probably be investing in a low-cost index tracker instead, but realistically that won't be the outcome that many will follow. Likewise, although there are successful technical investors out there, attempts to systemise technical indicators so that they can be statistically replicated always seem to fail. Just because a personality test suggests you would fit the profile of a technical investor doesn't mean you can find a profitable trading system.

The main issue with applying the categorisation that Meyers uses to your investment practice, however, is that it doesn't readily align with the type of categories that investors typically use to describe themselves. When asking individual investors what type of investor they are, I have never known anyone answer with one of the categories that Meyers uses. Instead, experienced investors tend to categorise themselves into one of four major types: Value, Momentum (or Trend), Quality, or Growth. I don't think this is a coincidence since these are based on the investment factors that are well-known in the academic literature to have generated historic outperformance over long periods.[13] (Technically, growth investing, as defined by high price-to-book or similar metrics, has historically underperformed as an investment factor. However, it is earnings growth that almost always ends up generating returns for investors, and there are many successful growth investors who buck the trend.) Investors tend to use these descriptions because they are well-known strategies that have been successful over time.

Some investors may employ a mix of these styles. Indeed, quant investors often try to generate excess returns using all these factors. Most individual investors are likely to favour one over the others, though, primarily because that style best fits their personality. Investors may also apply other labels to their investing style, but they often fall into one of these broad categories. For example, *income investors*, who focus on a high, sustainable and growing yield as the primary basis of their returns, are in effect taking advantage of the Value factor. Since dividends must be paid out of free cash flows which are generated through earnings over the long term, a high *sustainable* dividend yield must represent a low price-to-earnings or price-to-free cash flow, both characteristics of value stocks. In these cases, the psychological make-up required to stick with the strategy and the common mistakes are the same. Hence I don't break these additional types of investment strategy out separately.

Some of the biggest disagreements over investment strategy come from an inability to see outside of the lens in which we view the investment world. In reality, it doesn't matter which style of investor you are. What matters is that you are consistent, you recognise the strengths and weaknesses of that style, and you take steps to mitigate those weaknesses. In the rest of this chapter, I describe the four major investor types, the typical psychology of successful investors of that type and how that psychology may lead to certain common mistakes. If you don't yet know what type of investor you are, this chapter may help you to find your preferred style.

Value Investors

For value investors valuation is king. They look for a wide gap between the current share price and a conservative estimate of the intrinsic value of a business, based on known factors such as balance sheet entries or recurring revenues. They often choose to ignore all other investment information such as recent share price history or bad news about a company. In fact, in order to get the wide discount to their estimate of intrinsic value, value investors actively seek out shares hitting 52-week lows or with bad news in the press.[14] As discussed in Chapter 1, 'Competitive Advantage', value investors are looking to take advantage of mean reversion in corporate performance: struggling companies being pushed by their owners to improve their efficiency, reduce their working capital, invest in better products, or shut down unprofitable business lines. Some value investors may focus on buying stocks that trade at a significant discount to *Tangible Book Value*: the value of all of the company's tangible assets minus all its liabilities. Liquidating a business to realise that asset value is rarely a good move though: the costs of closing a business such as redundancy payments or indemnity insurance can make such a liquidation unprofitable. The discount to Tangible Book Value does indicate that those assets are currently unproductive, so increases the pressure on a company's management to put the resources to better use in generating earnings.

Psychology

Value investors are often described as contrarian: they are happy to go against the flow. They are bargain hunters who are not embarrassed to search the reduced aisle, or negotiate to get a reduced price. To be able to buy the stocks that everyone else hates they have to feel comfortable going their own way. Their personality often has a certain amount of *disagreeableness* in it. When they believe they are right, they are happy to shun the views of others and trust in their own judgement.

In personality psychology, *agreeableness* is one of the five major dimensions of personality structure.[15] People who are high in agreeableness have behavioural characteristics that are perceived as kind, considerate or sympathetic. A low level of agreeableness, i.e. *disagreeableness*, is not usually considered a good trait. It can relate to a lack of empathy, which may make it hard to develop strong relationships in life. It does mean, however, that those who have high levels of disagreeableness do not overly feel the need to be validated by others. According to author and podcaster Malcolm Gladwell, it is the personality trait of disagreeableness that enabled some of the greatest innovators, business leaders, or sportspeople to go against the conventional wisdom and develop new ideas that would have been rejected by those more reliant on the validation of others.[16] Likewise, those who have aspects of disagreeableness in their personality are more willing to hold the contrarian views necessary to be a successful value investor. Those who are highly agreeable may find it hard to go against the flow and buy unloved securities, even when their analysis shows that a stock is likely to be undervalued.

Common Mistakes

Given that being a value investor means going against the crowd, then a certain amount of self-belief and considerable patience is required. This can easily descend into stubbornness, with value investors failing to spot when the investment story has changed. Being able to respond to changing information by changing your mind is a critical component of being a successful investor. For this reason, value investors should take special note of rules on position sizing to avoid adding too much to losing positions; see Chapter 7, 'Overcoming Overconfidence'. Because they may be at risk of failing to recognise when the investment case has changed for the worse, value investors should also pay particular heed to the methods described in Chapter 10, 'Overcoming Commitment Bias'.

Value investors also tend to sell out of winning positions too soon. Since they are usually conservative in their assessment of intrinsic value, they demand a large margin of safety. However, when a company's prospects start to turnaround, there can be a significant positive impact on the intrinsic value of the company that isn't always immediately reflected in the published financial statements. The value investor needs to make sure they are re-assessing their estimate of intrinsic value as the story changes and have not become *anchored* on the original low price they bought at.

Value investors also have a strong desire to get a bargain, which means they may become overly focussed on buying at the very bottom. Since it is highly unlikely that an investor will buy at the bottom and sell at the top, this may cause the investor to miss a great trade simply because the stock has gone up a few per cent from its recent lows. Again, anchoring is causing the misstep here. See Chapter 12, 'Maintaining an Optimal Portfolio' for more information on overcoming this common error.

Momentum Investors

For momentum investors price action is king. They are taking advantage of the tendency of companies that are doing well to keep doing well, and those that are doing badly to keep doing badly. A typical momentum strategy looks at the share price performance from 12 months ago to one month ago. (In the very short term, one month or less, share prices tend to mean revert, so the most successful strategies ignore the last month's returns in their calculations.)[17] A market neutral strategy buys the top performers and shorts the worst performers, but momentum can be implemented successfully on the long side only.

Although momentum is implemented purely based on price action, it is generally accepted that it occurs due to under-reaction to fundamental changes in company performance. This may be due to a psychological bias where investors don't like to buy something they could have bought more cheaply earlier; buying at all-time highs may generate a feeling of regret that they didn't buy in sooner. To avoid regret, they don't buy at all, and may even stop following the company altogether. A simple strategy of buying shares that are at their 52-week highs has also historically generated outperformance, backing up the idea that this effect is probably due to investor under-reaction caused by regret.[18]

The momentum effect may also be due to the under-reaction of company management to changes in their business. If a business is generating higher than normal sales growth or profitability, it is natural for managers to try to keep some of that performance in reserve to even out their reporting. Equally, the management of companies that are performing badly may *travel hopefully*, refusing to accept the full weight of what has gone wrong. There is an old stock market adage that says 'profit warnings always come in threes', which nicely captures the tendency of management to under-react to adverse changes in business prospects as well as investors.

Momentum is also found in earnings as well as price action, which also suggests this effect is due to the under-reaction of investors and company managements to business trends. A combined strategy of price and earnings momentum has historically generated a higher return than price momentum alone.[19]

Psychology

Successful momentum investors have to be willing to buy something that has already gone up a lot, which means they will have to deal well with feelings of regret. It is quite natural for investors to feel that they should have bought the stock earlier and therefore never buy, due to those feelings. To take advantage of momentum, however, one must be willing to buy after share price increases.

Momentum investors also have to be able to live with periods of sharp reversal. The strategy will stop working rapidly but for relatively short periods of time. For example, a pure momentum strategy recorded a disastrous year in 2009 with more than 80% drawdown.[20] This can be difficult to bear for investors, not just because of the magnitude of the drawdown, but because of how quickly this occurs and the feeling of lack of control this can engender.

Compared to value investors, momentum investors are more likely to have an agreeable personality and be more comfortable going with the flow rather than against it. Successful momentum investors must also have a certain amount of humility. They are happy to admit that they don't know everything about a company and are willing to base investment decisions mainly on price action. Likewise, when the momentum fades, they don't ask why, they just get out.

Common Mistakes

Being a successful momentum investor requires not just successfully identifying stocks with momentum but selling when momentum fades. This may require selling a losing position, which is often difficult for investors, (see Chapter 8, 'Overcoming Loss Aversion'). One of the other significant challenges of being a momentum investor is selling winning stocks when the momentum is gone. For momentum investors, a successful investment will be one of their larger positions and may have made them large amounts of money. Over an extended holding period, the investor may increasingly appreciate the company's management and products. The risk is that they fall in love with the company and start to make investment decisions based on factors that are no longer related to the share price momentum to justify continuing to hold the stock. For pure momentum investors, relying on other investment factors apart from simple price momentum is often a mistake.

Gary Antonacci came up with the concept of dual momentum, which combines relative strength price momentum with absolute momentum, which is a form of trend following. Antonacci says that one of the mistakes momentum investors make is thinking that making a momentum strategy more complex adds value.[21] Although the momentum factor that is detailed in academic studies goes long stocks with the strongest medium-term price increase, and shorts stocks with the largest medium-term price decrease, a long-only momentum strategy delivers almost all of the long-term returns with added simplicity. A long-only strategy may also avoid some of the worst draw-downs of a momentum strategy, which typically occur as the general market trend reverses. Those who were short losing stocks when the market bottomed in March 2009 faced a period of significant losses since the weakest stocks rebounded most strongly.

Quality Investors

Quality investors are looking to find companies with sustainable competitive advantages, or *moats*, that prevent competitors from attacking their supra-normal profit margins. These types of companies will have brands, network effects, monopolies or other properties that provide their moats. Quality investors rely on the market failing to effectively price the potential future growth that having a strong and sustainable competitive advantage can bring. They often look for companies with high and sustainable corporate metrics, such as return on invested capital, to help them identify such moats.

One of the challenges of Quality Investing is that no moat is unbreachable. For example, over the last century, brands have provided a strong moat. The theory is that brands reduce search costs for consumers; with many decisions to make each day, consumers are happy to pay a little bit more to buy a product with a brand they trust and avoid having to weigh up the pros and cons of all the purchasing options. With the rise of online shopping, however, having good customer reviews can become more important than a recognisable brand, since this is another trusted way of reducing search costs. It is the companies that provide the platform, such as Amazon, that increasingly appear to have the competitive advantage, not the brand owners. A moat can also be allowed to be attacked, or sometimes even destroyed, by a careless management team. One of the most infamous accounts of brand-destruction was when Gerald Ratner publicly described his jewellery brand as 'crap' and hence almost instantly removed any value contained within the brand.[22] Other shifts in competitive advantage are subtler: for example, *Gillette* made their product too expensive, effectively over-pricing the value of their brand to reduce search costs and hence allowed an opportunity for the likes of *Dollar Shave Club* to get a foothold in the market. Likewise, *Schweppes* failed to adapt to the industry trends towards premiumisation within their drink mixer market and left the door open for *Fever-Tree* to take significant high-margin market share.

Despite these risks, when quality investors find a company with a sustainable competitive advantage, a long *runway* of available markets to expand into, which is selling at a reasonable price, it is likely to be an excellent investment. With these factors in place, the ability to re-invest capital at high rates over the very long term will generate exceptional returns to investors. Finding such companies before the market recognises them is hard though; quality investing requires significant analytical skill, not just in analysing financial metrics, but in understanding the nature of businesses and their place in the competitive marketplace.

Psychology

Successful Quality investors require high levels of *conscientiousness*: another of the five traits typically used to assess personality. Conscientious people have high levels of self-discipline and prefer to methodical planning to spontaneous action. Their ability to control, regulate and direct their impulses means that conscientious people are often highly successful in their chosen fields.

Finding companies that genuinely have a sustainable competitive advantage, a large market to address and where the market price does not already reflect these qualities is very rare. The returns to this strategy occur at an indeterminate time, over the very long term. Whereas a value investor is usually looking for mean reversion in the performance of a business to occur in an average period of 5 years or so, the quality investor is hoping to see above-market returns from a stock pick for 20 years or more. During this length of time, there will be a multitude of stock-specific events and market cycles. It will take great patience and self-discipline to ignore the noise of short-term corporate performance and instead focus on the quality of the moat and the size of the addressable market. Conscientiousness gives quality investors the immense patience required to find and stick with long-term winning companies.

Common Mistakes

Since markets are highly competitive, being a quality investor requires very strong analytical skills. You cannot rely solely on simple metrics, such as return on capital, to identify quality companies. Although these may signify a company that has a sustainable competitive advantage, they could equally indicate a company that is in the right place at the right time but where competitors are quickly catching up. Recall that return on capital mean reverts for most companies. If a quality investor purchases a stock with a high return on capital and it reverts to the mean, they will almost certainly lose a considerable amount of money. Quality investors need to be able to continually and dispassionately assess the strength of the moat of the companies that they hold, as well as that of potential investments.

In his book, *100 baggers*, Christopher Mayer analysed companies whose share price has gone up 100-fold over time.[23] These are the sort of companies that quality investors are looking to find, and such stellar returns, even in a single stock, will generate significant profit for any portfolio. While owning a 100 bagger sounds great in hindsight, there are some reasons why this may be problematic in real life. The first is that such stellar returns will see this stock dominate your portfolio and, as I explain in Chapter 7, 'Overcoming Overconfidence', this is unlikely to be wise. The second is that all the 100 baggers that Mayer studied had significant drawdowns, often as large as 50%. Few people are able to behave rationally when they have a substantial proportion of their wealth in a single stock and it goes down 50%. This is what is required to generate outperformance as a Quality investor, though: an ability to ignore price action and focus on the strength and sustainability of competitive advantage.

Growth Investors

Growth investors recognise that a company with rapidly growing revenue is likely to produce significant profits in the future, even if it is loss-making now. If those rates of growth continue, then due to positive operational gearing, considerable profit growth often follows. The challenge of growth investing is that the market, on average, over-pays for growth. It is not enough to identify a company that has the potential to grow at, say, 30% per annum, you have to identify a company that has the potential to grow at 30% per annum but is priced as if it is going to grow at 20% per annum. If you pay a price that assumes it will grow at 40% per annum, you will lose money even if it grows at 30% per annum.

One of the popular metrics amongst growth investors is the Price-Earnings Growth ratio, or PEG, which was popularised by Peter Lynch and Jim Slater.[24][25] This is usually calculated by taking the forward (next year's predicted) Price-Earnings ratio and dividing it by the expected growth rate in earnings. The idea is that since you should be willing, all else being equal, to pay a higher Price-Earnings ratio for a stock that is growing more rapidly, so a low PEG may represent an undervalued stock. Of course, analysing the growth potential of companies requires significantly more in-depth analysis than a simple metric, but it may form a good starting point to identify candidates for further research.

Psychology

The psychological traits of growth investors, as measured by the usual psychological tests, are probably more diverse than those of Value, Quality or Momentum investors. There appears to be no strong correlation between the big five personality traits and the characteristics that one needs to stick with a successful growth investing strategy. We do get, however, some clues about what may be required from the Cronqvist research into the investment styles of twins:[26]

> ...we find that investors with more human capital in the form of more education and higher levels of labor income prefer growth stocks, as do investors whose labor income covaries more positively with GDP growth. That is, investors whose labor income is reduced in bad states of the world prefer growth over value stocks.

Cronqvist also found that Growth investors tend to be younger and have more disposable income than their more Value-orientated peers. Although he doesn't make an explicit link to personality in his study, there appears to be one common factor in those findings: optimism. To be a growth investor, it seems, you have to be optimistic, both about your prospects and the future in general. In most countries, optimism declines with age, and it is easy to see how those with more disposable income would view their future more positively. They are more willing to invest in a way that maximises their return from an increasingly positive future.

Common Mistakes

Since most Growth investors will be optimistic, they will be particularly susceptible to the mistakes caused by optimism bias. They should be particularly wary of falling for frauds, unwittingly buying into fads, or investing in financially weak companies. Growth investors would particularly benefit from developing checklists that filter out companies at risk of being frauds, fads, or failures. Chapter 9, 'Overcoming Optimism Bias', will help investors do that.

The other mistake that Growth investors make is overpaying for earnings growth. Historically, investing in a basket of growth stocks, as defined by simple metrics such as high price-to-book, is a losing strategy; on average, the market over-values growth. The successful growth investor has to ask themselves not just 'why will this company grow quickly?' but 'why will this company grow more quickly than the market currently expects?'

Growth stocks often have great stories attached to them of how they are going to change an industry, or even the world, for the better. It can be hard not to get excessively caught up in such narratives. Chapter 9 also provides some ways of dealing with this common problem.

This brings us to the end of our look at the common investment styles, but before we end Part One, it pays to introduce one of the most contentious topics in investing, one where different investment styles can have radically different practices: should you average down, or not?

Averaging Down

Averaging down means adding to a losing investment so that your average buy price is reduced. Raising this topic in an investment discussion can be like pulling the pin from a hand grenade and standing back. Some great investors hold strong opposing opinions on this topic and their views are widely quoted. For example:

> I must say, I NEVER have put in a stop loss order because if you like a stock and buy it and it goes down, then you should buy more if you can afford it.[27]
>
> Walter Schloss

> Always sell what shows you a loss and keep what shows you a profit.[28]
>
> Jesse Livermore

> ...a price drop [is] as an opportunity to load up on bargains from amongst your worst performers...a price drop in a good stock is only a tragedy if you sell at that price and never buy more.[29]
>
> Peter Lynch

> In fact, when we own portions of outstanding businesses with outstanding managements, our favorite holding period is forever. We are just the opposite of those who hurry to sell and book profits when companies perform well but who tenaciously hang on to businesses that disappoint. Peter Lynch aptly likens such behavior to cutting the flowers and watering the weeds.[30]
>
> Warren Buffet

One of the mistakes investors can make when reading these quotes is to interpret them as strict rules to be obeyed in all situations. They often miss the caveats contained within them. Lynch says a price drop in 'a good stock' is an opportunity, not a price drop per se. Although it is Buffett who is most associated with the maxim, 'Don't garden by digging up the flowers and watering the weeds', he is actually quoting Peter Lynch, who suggests averaging down in good stocks. It would seem that Lynch and Buffett's 'flowers' are well-performing *businesses* with sound economics, and their 'weeds' are badly-performing *businesses*. Furthermore, Buffett averaged down on Coca Cola, which is strong evidence that he is not recommending making such decisions purely on price action. In this light, we should avoid narrowly interpreting averaging down as a good or bad practice. The key is to find an investment practice for losing investments that aligns with your personality and investment strategy.

The other issue with saying one is *averaging down* is it suggests that your current average buy price matters. It does not. To the completely rational investor, the price that they bought a stock at is entirely irrelevant. A rational investor asks themselves 'given all current known information do I have the right position size?' not 'should I average down?' Unfortunately, as Part Two will show, we are far from fully rational, which means having a strategy for how you deal with the *average-down dilemma* will be one of the key parts of *knowing yourself*.

Lee Freeman-Shor, in his book *The Art of Execution*, analysed 31,000 trades of 45 professional investors.[31] He found that how one responded to price declines was one of the critical factors in determining which investors made money over the long term. He split the investors into three categories: *Assassins*, *Hunters* and *Rabbits*.

Assassins always had a stop-loss and killed a losing investment before it did any real damage, selling when the price dropped by 20-30%. The *Assassins*' discipline paid off: they tended to be profitable investors overall, particularly if they were able to hold onto their winning investments so that they benefitted fully from their successful trades.

Hunters had a completely different approach and bought more of an investment as it declined. They also tended to be investors who made money overall. Their ability to add to losing positions often generated a profit on an investment even if the price of the stock never rose above their original buy price.

Rabbits were those investors for whom a losing investment froze them in the headlights and they took no action at all. Unfortunately, the *Rabbits* mostly ended up as losing investors, run over by the market. It seems there is no ideal rule for responding to price declines, but it is crucial that you develop an active strategy that avoids becoming a *Rabbit*.

Will you be an *Assassin* or a *Hunter*?

You may already have a good feel for which type you should be. As I mentioned, investors often have strong feelings about averaging down, which is a sign that many already have found a fit with their personality. As a generalisation, you may find that Value and Quality investors are more prone to being *Hunters*, and Growth and Momentum investors are more likely to be *Assassins* but the split is far from absolute.

If you are not sure which would fit you best, then take some time to analyse your past losing investments, particularly ones where you ended up as the *Rabbit* in the headlights. It was by analysing the losing trades of the portfolio managers to whom he allocated capital, that Freeman-Shor identified these winning and losing styles of behaviour. By doing the same, you may get some insight into what strategy would fit you best.

One final warning before we leave this topic: if you most closely associate yourself with a *Hunter*, one who buys more of an investment as it declines, there are some times where averaging down is *not* a good strategy. Australian hedge fund manager John Hempton has looked extensively at when value investors should average down and he cautions that they should avoid doing so where the company has significant financial or operational leverage.[32]

Consider the cautionary tale of Bill Miller, who was once considered one of the greatest value investors around. The fund he ran, Legg Mason Capital Management Value Trust, beat the S&P 500 index, after fees, for 15 consecutive years from 1991 through 2005.[33] However, subsequent to 2006 he lost his investors all the previous cumulative outperformance, primarily by continuing to average down on companies such as American International Group, Wachovia, Washington Mutual, Freddie Mac, Countrywide Financial and Citigroup, as they declined in the Great Financial Crisis.[34] The common factor amongst these stocks is that they all have significant leverage. Looking at that list of rogues, if governments and central banks hadn't intervened at the nadir of the crisis, Bill Miller's record would have been even worse.

Another reason to avoid averaging down in companies that have high leverage is that in such companies, managers are highly incentivised not to reveal the true extent of any issues to the market. Their debt will come with covenants attached to protect the lender and the apparent strength of the business may determine the ability of the company to raise additional equity from the market. When in distress, management will want to present the rosiest picture possible to lenders and shareholders. Like Wile E. Coyote running off the edge of a cliff, they may keep their legs moving in vain hope, until gravity eventually brings them back to earth.

The second category that Hempton cautions against averaging down on is companies that are suffering from technical obsolescence, for example, Kodak. As film cameras became replaced by digital ones, Kodak faced a market for film that was in permanent decline. Well-managed companies in an industry that is declining may make good investments; the market often under-estimates the time required for fundamental industry changes to occur and a declining industry discourages new entrants, leaving incumbent companies higher profit margins. However, there is always a possibility that the performance of the company will continue to decline and go to zero. Hence these are not the sort of stocks where averaging down makes sense.

As we come to the end of Part One, you should have a better idea of the type of investor you are and what investment style fits your unique set of skills and personality. You will understand what your competitive advantages are as an investor and will be in a position to make sure you only invest where *you* have the advantage. Even though you are now playing with the upper hand, there are still ways in which you can lose. Sometimes unforeseen circumstances overwhelm your advantage, but it is often the unforced errors that cause the biggest losses. I look at some of these potential errors in Part Two, and more importantly, how to avoid them.

Part Two

Overcome Your Weaknesses

6
Behavioural Biases

Behavioural biases occur when we consistently make sub-optimal decisions due to an inability to assess the information we possess correctly. This is not the problem of incomplete information, where an unpredictable event causes a company to perform unexpectedly badly, it is when we have all the information that we need to make a good decision, but we still make a poor one.

Up until the 1970s social scientists generally took the view that human decision-making was mostly rational and that any deviation from rationality was due to excessively emotional responses. The behaviour of financial markets has a tendency to elicit strong emotions in us. Remaining unemotional while experiencing fortune and misfortune on a daily basis, seeing our wealth fluctuate by measurable amounts in seconds, is impossible for most people. While excessive emotion will undoubtedly lead to poor decision-making and financial markets are particularly good at evoking strong emotions, the role of emotion in decision-making is complex.

Strangely, it seems that some emotional engagement is required for a successful decision-making process. We know this from the study of patients who, due to accident or disease, have had the part of their brain that processes emotional responses disconnected from the part of their brain that makes conscious decisions. You would think that these people who are unable to be guided by their emotions would be some kind of decision superheroes: like Mr Spock, from the Star Trek series, they would be driven to make optimal decisions through the application of pure logic alone. Instead, we see the opposite. Without the guiding hand of emotions, these unfortunate people are unable to make *any* decisions.

Neurologist Antonio Damasio describes the impact that this condition had on one such patient.[1] As part of his treatment, he gave the patient the option of two alternative dates for a follow-up appointment. They were both in the coming month, a few days apart from each other. The patient opened their appointment book and then proceeded to debate with themselves for almost half an hour as to the pros and cons of each option. The patient's lengthy cost-benefit analysis included not just proximity to other engagements but long-range weather forecasts, traffic conditions and all manner of other potential factors. So maddening was the behaviour, Damasio describes having to force himself to observe the process and not intervene to force the patient to make a decision.

This presents a problem for our investment decisions. We cannot simply untangle our emotions from our decision-making process, and even if it were possible it might leave us unable to make any decisions at all, like those brain-damaged patients.

It's not just excessive emotions that can lead us astray too. In the late 1970s Professor Daniel Kahneman, the Nobel Prize-winning psychologist, together with fellow Israeli, Amos Tversky, started to document a series of biases in decision-making that appeared to be unrelated to emotional responses.[2] Instead, these biases were traced to how our brains conduct the decision-making process by using mental shortcuts known as *heuristics*.

An example of a common heuristic is what is known as *social proof*: when we face uncertainty in a decision, we look to what others are doing to guide us.[3] Imagine you are on holiday in a small town and you are looking for a place to eat dinner. As you enter the square in the centre of the town you see two restaurants, one almost full, and one mostly empty.

Where would you choose to eat?

Most of the time, the busy restaurant will be the better one. Since some people will be in-the-know and will have consciously chosen the best restaurant it will be busier. The social proof heuristic would usually be a good way of making this decision. However, it is certainly possible that the first people to enter the square that night randomly chose the now busy restaurant and social proof led all the other diners to eat there, whatever the merits of the now empty restaurant. Note that restauranteurs know very well the power of social proof, which is why they always try to seat you in the window if you are the first to arrive. (Of course, with the advent of *Trip Advisor* the power of physical social proof in the restaurant industry is reduced, or at least replaced with online social proof.)

Applying this heuristic to our decision-making is largely subconscious. It is this automatic processing that advertisers play on with slogans such as '8 out of 10 cats prefer Whiskas' or 'The UK's number one…' These simple appeals to social proof are surprisingly good at influencing our buying decisions because using social proof is usually a good way of making a decision.

The problem is that using such intuitive judgements to assess the relative likelihood of *complex* situations is more likely to lead us astray than to guide us. We appear to be poor natural statisticians. In Kahneman's experiments, even professional statisticians made poor intuitive judgements about statistics. Investment decisions are particularly prone to error since these almost always require logical and statistical analysis. These errors in judgement are not random, though; when we make mistakes, we tend to do so in a predictable manner. It turns out that our behaviour ends up *consistently* biased.

To explain the behavioural biases we all suffer from, psychologists such as Kahneman have created a model that aims to explain how our brains process information. This model separates the type of information processing our brains conduct into two systems.[4] The first is called *System 1*. It is quick, reactive and always on. It makes rapid decisions in situations where speed of processing is important. System 1 thinking is valuable because it can quickly and easily assess a threat and take appropriate action. As well as being able to make decisions quickly, it reduces the cognitive load required to make every-day decisions. It is System 1 that uses heuristics, subconscious rules of thumb, to make good simple decisions the majority of the time.

The second type of thinking process is called *System 2*. It is slower, more deliberate, and more thorough. While System 1 thinking is great for making quick decisions on trivial options, such as 'do I want ice cream or custard with that?', it generally makes poor decisions when it automatically weighs in on complex topics.

In his classic work, Kahneman references the following example of how System 1 thinking can lead us astray.[5] Consider the problem:

> A bat and Ball cost £1.10. The bat costs £1 more than a ball, how much does the ball cost?

For many people, their System 1 immediately takes one from the other and answers 10p. Unless you have heard this problem before, the same instinctive answer probably came to mind immediately for you. If you have heard the problem before, or have enough experience to be suspicious of apparently simple questions in books on psychology, you will know the answer is not quite as straightforward, and this will have acted as a prompt for you to engage your System 2 thinking. Those who do engage their System 2 thinking get the right answer easily by doing the maths:

Bat + ball = £1.10, and Bat − Ball = £1.00

So, Bat = £1.00 + Ball

So, £1.00 + Ball + Ball = £1.10

So, 2 x Ball = £0.10

So, Ball = £0.05

Good investment decision requires deliberate and methodical System 2 thinking. If we recognise that investing falls into this type of thinking, maybe we can prevent our System 1 jumping in with wrong conclusions.

The challenge is that our System 1 is always active, making quick reactive judgements on everything we perceive. To engage our System 2 to make a good investment decision we must *over-rule* our System 1, which has already provided a quick, intuitive decision. Over-ruling our System 1 when it has already provided an answer can be quite hard to do. Even if you knew that the answer to the bat and ball problem was not straightforward, your System 1 still provided the immediate, intuitive but wrong answer. It is only your experience or suspicion that enabled you to quickly reject this and engage your System 2 to come up with the right solution. There will be plenty of situations where you are not sufficiently experienced or suitably suspicious and instead accept the wrong intuitive judgement.

There is another reason why we may not use our System 2 as often as we would like: it requires significantly more mental effort than System 1. System 2 thinking is a function of a part of our brain called the *prefrontal cortex,* which uses a large amount of energy. For this reason, our body doesn't like to use this unnecessarily. In one study, by psychologist Dr Roy Baumeister, students were asked to complete a mentally challenging task: watching a video while ignoring words that flashed up on the screen.[6] (It takes effort to ignore stimuli as well as respond to them.) After the task, students were given a drink of lemonade. Half of the drinks contained sugar and half were a sugar-free variety. After waiting for about 15 minutes, giving the sugar time to enter their bloodstream, the students were asked to make a decision about a future preference for living arrangements. Baumeister found that the students who had been given the sugar-free drink made less rational decisions; they relied much more on instinct and intuition in their decision-making process. It seems that we find it harder to engage the mental processes of our System 2, and therefore make less rational decisions, when we have low blood sugar. For this reason, investment decisions are better made when we are not hungry.

Although being hungry may lead to poor investment decision-making, being tired almost certainly will. A study by Professor John Medina from University of Washington School of Medicine showed that if an A-student, used to scoring top 10% in their studies, gets under seven hours of sleep on weekdays, she will begin to score in the bottom 9% of non-sleep-deprived individuals.[7] In another study by Dr David Dinges at the University of Pennsylvania, after two weeks of six hours of sleep a night, study participants were shown to have similar brain function to people who were drunk.[8] After two weeks of four hours of sleep a night, participants were unable to function effectively at all.

The most worrying thing about the study was that sleep-deprived individuals were unable to realise their own lack of function. Most reported that they were 'tired but ok'. This may be due to what is known as the *Dunning-Kruger effect*: where the skills required to detect competency are the same as actually being competent.[9] The lack of sleep had removed not only competency from the subjects but the ability to detect competency in themselves or others.

It is also worth mentioning that alcohol inhibits the functioning of the prefrontal cortex too.[10] So it is best not to make any investment decisions under the influence either. You may find yourself failing to engage your System 2 thinking process as much as you would like.

Knowing that our System 1 makes poor intuitive investment decisions, we can choose to consciously engage our System 2. This is possible, just as it is possible to do the maths to come up with the right answer in the bat and ball puzzle (and will be easier if you are not tired, hungry or drunk). However, anyone who has tried to lose weight or give up a bad habit knows how ineffective knowledge alone is at changing behaviour. Knowing that salad is better for you often doesn't help you choose it when you are hungry and there's pizza on the menu. If Kahneman reports that all of his research into behavioural biases has not been effective at improving his personal decision-making, simply trying to avoid them is unlikely to be a successful strategy for you.

The academic research into behavioural biases does contain some good news, though: we are *predictably irrational*.[11] Because behavioural biases are consistent, you can identify the types of situations in which you will be most prone to poor decision-making. You can then make rules for your portfolio that will help to overcome these weaknesses: intentionally restricting your choices in situations where you know you have the greatest danger of being led astray by behavioural biases or excess emotion. When looking to lose weight, it is a lot easier to be disciplined by not buying chocolate in the supermarket, than not eating it when you are hungry and it's within reach.

While using rules to restrict options doesn't sound like a route to optimal decision-making, it is not without precedent. In his book, *The Checklist Manifesto*, surgeon, Atul Gawande, describes how checklists have been used successfully in such diverse areas as medicine and aviation to prevent avoidable mistakes.[12] At first glance, the World Health Organisation checklist for surgery, that Gawande helped to develop, seems very simple.[13] It contains checks such as:

> Have all team members introduced themselves by name and role?
>
> Has the patient confirmed their identity?
>
> Is the operating site marked?
>
> Does the patient have any known allergies?

Could such simple checks really add value to the actions of a highly educated and trained surgery team?

They did. Three months after implementation of the checklist, 78% of operating room staff had observed the checklist prevent an operating error.[14] It generated these benefits by identifying the most common preventable mistakes made by surgical teams and putting in place rules or checks to systematically overcome these.

Another finding that may surprise you is, that when a decision-making process can be improved by using rules or checklists, experts tend to make poorer decisions than non-experts. In one example from Michael Lewis's book, *The Undoing Project*, oncology experts were asked how they would identify if an x-ray of a patient's gastric ulcer was likely to reveal cancerous growth.[15] All the experts were able to articulate the number and relevance of the factors that one would use to make a good diagnosis. However, when they were shown a series of real x-rays, where the outcome was already known by the researchers, they were unable to apply their knowledge to make accurate diagnoses. They didn't follow their own methodology, overruling it when non-predictive factors appeared that seemed relevant. When first-year residents were given the oncology experts' list of factors to use in diagnosing the x-rays they performed much better than the experts themselves. It seems the experts applied their personal judgement to overrule the known factors too many times, whereas the residents rigidly applied the rubric and made better diagnoses.

The risk then is that, even if you make good rules to overcome behavioural bias in your portfolio, as your expertise increases you will be increasingly tempted to overrule them with your personal judgement. The studies of expert judgement suggest that you should not, and that if you do so you will make worse decisions overall.

At the most extreme, people have used the idea of permanently restricting their choices to drive them toward the behaviours and goals they want to achieve. On landing in South America in 1519, Cortes intentionally burnt his ships. For him, retreat was not an option; he had to move forward to his goal or die trying. In the Cold War, the concept of Mutually Assured Destruction held the same power. Since both NATO and the Eastern Bloc knew that any attack would lead to an automatic response of retaliation that would destroy them too, they would not willingly start an attack. Such a policy only works where the retaliation is not optional.

While going to these lengths may be a bit too severe for investment decisions, it does show what a powerful impact intentionally restricting your choices can have on decision-making and achieving the desired outcome. Make good rules and stick to them.

In this vein, the next four chapters describe some of the most powerful and pervasive behavioural biases that affect investment decisions and rules that you can apply to avoid the destruction of your portfolio.

7
Overcoming Overconfidence

Almost everyone is overconfident. When polled, 80% of people consider themselves a better-than-average driver.[1] If you don't think *you* are overconfident, then that is probably because you are overconfident about it.

Being positive about our abilities makes sense. We would struggle to get out of bed, build businesses, make friends, or raise families if we consistently dwelled on the chances that we would regularly fail along the way. The only group of people who appear to not suffer from overconfidence are the clinically depressed. I suspect that is a trade-off that none of us would be willing to accept.

One way to temper your overconfidence in your investment practice (or life) would be to keep a record of all the events you think are almost certain to happen and then review later to see how many actually happened. I think most of us would find that far fewer occurred than we expected. The problem is that, even when we have objective evidence of our overconfidence in our own handwriting, we often add a narrative to past events that simply wasn't there at the time. When something we predicted didn't happen, we say to ourselves 'actually, I knew that prediction was risky' or 'it would have happened but another unforeseen event happened'. We let ourselves off the hook too many times. Even with a real record of our successes and failures, it is tough to separate luck from skill in any individual investment outcome. While keeping good records of *why* you bought or sold a stock is likely to add value to your process, it is unlikely to cure you of your overconfidence.

Overconfidence is so common in military engagements that it has its own name: Victory Disease. This is where a series of victories gives a commander so much confidence in the skill of his command and the ability of his troops that he makes a subsequent engagement that proves disastrous. In most cases, the fatal campaign occurs despite very strong prior evidence from intelligence reports that it was likely to fail.

Napoleon decided to invade Russia without the logistical ability to fight a sustained campaign, based on a false belief that Russia would quickly surrender.[2] General Custer didn't seek, or ignored, intelligence that suggested the *Battle for Little Big Horn* was not going to be a comfortable victory like his previous engagement with the Cheyenne at the *Battle of Washita River*.[3] In the Second World War the United States failed to respond to intelligence reports that suggested war with Japan was imminent, and although they had war-gamed an attack on Pearl Harbour it wasn't taken seriously, so they were not in the habit of sending out reconnaissance planes to give advance warning of any attack.[4]

The Japanese then suffered from victory disease themselves, as their nearly uninterrupted victories in the Pacific encouraged them to abandon defensive plans and continue to expand beyond where their logistical capacity could properly support their navy. This led to catastrophic defeat in the Battle of Midway in 1942 and the sinking of four Japanese aircraft carriers.[5] Overconfidence, it seems, casts a long shadow on history as well as our investment practice.

Overconfidence in investing becomes a problem when you are too sure about what you know. You overweight the probabilities of positive events happening and then make wrong investment decisions based on those probabilities.

Maybe doing more research, and therefore reducing the number of unknowns about your investments, is the answer?

In a famous experiment, now over 50 years old, a clinical psychologist gathered other psychologists together to review a number of patient cases.[6] The psychologists were given an initial set of information about a patient and asked to answer 25 questions about their personality or motivations. Since we humans are complex beings, getting an accurate psychological assessment of a patient is a difficult task; with the initial set of information they got about 26% right. The psychologists were then asked to answer the same set of questions a further three times, each time they were given additional information about the patients. When the results were analysed, the additional information had no significant impact on the accuracy of their answers, which only rose by 2%. However, after they were given the fourth set of data, their confidence levels in their diagnoses had soared, from an initial level of around 33%, to 53%. The psychologists began their work 7% overconfident and ended up 25% overconfident due to the increased amount of information they were given.

Increased investment research may well have the same effect that more information did for these psychological assessments. Gaining a greater understanding of a company may improve your judgement about the merits of an investment, but it will also increase your confidence in your judgement, potentially more than the ability of the additional information to improve your decision-making. Therein lies the problem.

Trying to correct our overconfidence by conducting more research is also problematic because of how we tend to approach adding to our knowledge base. We suffer from *confirmation bias*, that is the tendency to seek out information that confirms our prior held beliefs, and a tendency to ignore or downplay information that contradicts them. You see this effect on social media: when it comes to a controversial topic we tend to *follow*, *like* and *share* those whose opinion we already agree with, and *block* or *mute* those we disagree with. This tendency makes it very hard to correct our overconfidence through better research; we probably aren't even looking in the right place to find a contrary opinion.

Overconfidence is also difficult to overcome because we are unaware of what we don't know, the so-called unknown unknowns. It is easy to know what you know about something, much harder to know what you don't know. By definition, unknown unknowns lie outside your current ability to perceive them. Often the life-threatening risks to a company come from the completely unpredictable. Take, for example, the list of the largest ever casino losses in Las Vegas from Nassim Taleb's book *The Black Swan*.[7] Casinos with good risk models are almost certain to make money in the long term; the odds are literally in their favour. They just have to avoid taking in bets that are too large compared to their capital, where a run of bad luck would bankrupt them. These risks can be effectively modelled, and casino bosses will step in to prevent gamblers betting more than the casino's limit. None of the largest casino losses feature gambling though; they are all due to completely unpredictable events. An employee, for no apparent reason, fails to submit paperwork to the Internal Revenue Service for years and no-one notices, yielding a massive fine; or one day, one of the tigers that they allowed to sleep in their bedrooms, decides to maim Roy Horn from the act Siegfried and Roy, triggering $100m of refunds and lawsuits.

It is no coincidence that a film about the overconfidence in ever-rising house prices, *The Big Short*, opens with the following quote:[8]

> It ain't what you don't know that gets you into trouble. It's what you know for sure that just ain't so.

With overconfidence so pervasive and difficult to counter, there is only one thing that can protect against it in your investing practice: diversify more than you think you need to.

Diversification is another one of the most controversial topics in investing. Warren Buffett has said that diversification makes no sense for those who know their investments well and suggests that most people would be better off investing their money in only their best ideas.[9] He introduced a concept of a 20-hole punch card, representing the 20 investments one can make in one's lifetime, as a way of improving investors' stock selection. While the concept of choosing one's investments very carefully rather than jumping in and out of whatever seems "hot" is undoubtedly a good one, I think there is a chance that even the great Buffett may have been overconfident on occasions.

When he ran the Buffett Partnership, the partnership rules allowed him to have up to 35% of his portfolio in one position. Over the five years to 1961 he built a controlling stake in a company called Dempster Mill, who made farm equipment.[10] He started buying at $17 per share and eventually built up a 70% stake at a $28 per share average price. This represented a significant discount to his conservative estimate of $35 per share in tangible assets. The stake in Dempster Mill accounted for 20% of the Partnership's funds. The problem was that the management of the company was resistant to change, and the already high inventories kept increasing, sucking in cash to fund working capital. Buffett had to get rid of the management to implement the changes he wanted, but when he did the company's bank became worried and threatened to seize the collateral backing its loan. If this company had gone into liquidation, with the bank seizing all the assets of the business, there was no guarantee that Buffett would receive anything back. Such situations have a habit of seeing little or no return to equity holders after the creditors are made whole and the administrators paid.

At this point, Charlie Munger introduced Buffett to a turnaround specialist called Harry Bottle, whom he hired on the spot. Bottle did make the necessary operational changes that the previous management was unwilling to make, the banks issued a stay of execution and he did turn the company around. It was sold for $80 a share.

Reflecting on the Dempster situation much later, Buffett states that if the bank's decision had gone the other way his wealth would have taken a significant hit:

> ...hiring Harry may have been the most important management decision I ever made. Dempster was in big trouble under the two previous managers, and the banks were treating us as a potential bankrupt. If Dempster had gone down, my life and fortunes would have been a lot different from that time forward.[11]

One of the objections to greater diversification is that the more stocks you own the more you end up tracking the broad stock market indexes. This idea comes from research in 1970 by Lawrence Fisher and James H. Lorie when they were looking into how many stocks you need to own to remove variability from a portfolio.[12] At that time, investors wanted exposure to the broad stock market but index funds and ETFs were not widely available, and the cost of maintaining a portfolio of hundreds of stocks was costly. Fisher and Lorie found that portfolios of just 32 stocks chosen at random removed 95% of the variability in the distribution of returns.

Investors often misinterpret this research to mean that if they own more than 30 stocks they are simply tracking the market. This misses a crucial point, though: stock-pickers are not choosing stocks randomly. If you have skill in stock-picking there is no reason that a portfolio of 30 or more stocks should track the market. Another issue with relying on the Fisher and Lorie study is the measure they used: the standard deviation of returns. A more recent study used the better measure of *tracking error* and found that even 60 randomly selected stocks only removed 88% of the tracking risk.[13]

As an example of highly diversified investors who still generate outperformance versus an index tracker, consider the so-called *quants*.

These investors will own hundreds of stocks, aiming to capture a premium that reflects a general mispricing amongst stocks with specific characteristics. They disavow stock-picking based on personal judgement and aim to take no stock-specific risk at all, often using computer models to do all the trading. Despite the high number of stocks owned, these quant funds don't just track the market because they don't choose stocks randomly but select them based on criteria that have shown to generate historical outperformance.

While it is possible to own too many stocks and not having enough time to research them thoroughly, overconfidence means that most investors suffer from under-diversification not over-diversification. There is no magic number that is the right number of stocks to own for all investors and all market conditions. In reality, each investor's strategy and circumstances will mean that their ideal level of diversification will vary significantly.

The following table gives some of the factors that you should consider when determining your ideal level of diversification:

More Concentrated	More Diversified
Conducting in-depth stock analysis	Relying on quant methods, or stock-picking with simple metrics, such as Price-Earnings ratios
Investing with smaller amounts of money	Investing with larger amounts of money
Earlier in life	Later in life
Experienced Investors	Novice Investors
Where you can influence or exercise control over an investment outcome	Where you have little or no influence over your invested companies
Have other sources of income	Reliant on investment performance for most living expenses.

Note how several of these factors can pull in opposite directions. When you are a novice investor you are more likely to be unaware of what you don't know, so should be more diversified. Yet you also are likely to be investing with smaller amounts of money and have a longer investment horizon, so are more able to ride out the impact of the unknown unknown events that will impact your portfolio.

Looking at the table, it makes sense why Buffett often ran a concentrated portfolio in his original fund, Buffett Partnership Limited. He was doing in-depth analysis, was experienced but still early in life and often exercised significant control over his investments. Not everyone is as fortunate as Buffett though.

While holding hundreds of stocks is likely to lead to the individual investor being unable to know their investments in sufficient detail, the consequences of being under-diversified are typically more severe. To demonstrate why, I need to introduce a bit of mathematical theory.

John L. Kelly Jr. was a pioneer in applying mathematics to betting games.[14] He developed what became known as the Kelly Criterion, which proves that in a series of bets you will always end up with the highest long-term compound return by betting the proportion of your bankroll (the total amount of capital you have to bet with) in proportion to your edge versus the odds you are offered. *Edge* in betting terms is how much you can expect to win, on average, over a large number of events. If you were successfully counting cards at Blackjack, for example, you might gain an advantage such that you would expect to win 51% of the time. Out of 100 bets, you would expect to come away with £10,200 (calculated by taking 51 winning bets where you receive £200 back and 49 losing bets where you receive nothing back), which means you win £2 for every £100 wagered. Your edge is 2%. The odds you are offered represent how much you win when you are right. In Blackjack, the house returns double your stake when you win, so the odds are 1:1. The Kelly Criterion says that to maximise the rate of return, you would bet 2% (calculated as your edge of 2% divided by your odds of 1) of the total amount of money you have to play with.

The concept of the Kelly Criterion was later adapted to include the case where you have many competing positive expectation bets, as you do in building an investment portfolio. I cover this in more detail in Part Three, but for the moment, what is important is what happens when you over-bet or under-bet versus the ideal Kelly proportion of your portfolio. That is, when you put a greater proportion of your portfolio into a stock than the Kelly Criterion suggests, or less.

It turns out that if you under-bet versus the Kelly proportion, you don't compound your wealth as fast, but the impact is slight, and it has the advantage of significantly reducing the drawdowns you face from bets that don't come in.

As would seem logical, the Kelly Criterion says that you should only accept positive expectation bets and refuse negative expectation bets; if your edge is negative the amount you should bet is negative, i.e. you should try and take the other side of the bet. Just because you are only making positive expectation bets doesn't mean you won't face a run of bad luck though. If you over-bet versus the Kelly proportion, there is an increasing chance that at some point in time you will wipe out, that is, lose almost all your wealth. The Kelly Criterion is a proportional betting system; you always bet a percentage of your current bankroll, not an absolute amount. So technically you can never lose all your money. This is of little consequence, however, to the investor who sees his portfolio go down to a non-zero but negligible amount. Over-betting occurs when people consistently over-estimate their edge, as one is likely to do if one is overconfident.

Using the Kelly Criterion to guide your position sizes, can be viewed as walking up a slope approaching a cliff edge. The higher that you end up at the end of the day, the higher your long-term wealth will be. If you had perfect visibility you would feel quite confident approaching close to the cliff edge to maximise your wealth. However, if visibility was reduced by fog you would be much more cautious. The consequences of going just slightly too far are much more severe than stopping a fair way short. Unlike betting games such as Blackjack, the odds that the stock market offers you, and your estimate of the edge that you have on an individual investment, are at best vague approximations. The fog is thick at the investing cliff edge and you should be suitably cautious.

Since you will have considerable uncertainty when assessing your edge and the odds you are offered, it is logical to reduce your bet size, which is equivalent to increasing your diversification. In doing so, you avoid the most significant drawdowns and the risk of an almost total loss, with only a small reduction in the long-term rate of portfolio return.

The one area that investors can end up over-diversified is when buying investment trusts or funds. Such investment vehicles are often highly diversified in themselves, so by holding many different funds, the investor ends up with a very broad portfolio. While there is nothing necessarily wrong with having that level of diversification, creating it via multiple managed funds is a very expensive way of doing this. Instead of paying 0.2% or less in annual fees for a global equity portfolio, investors end up paying 2% or more for essentially the same portfolio, virtually guaranteeing underperformance.

Portfolio Limits

The simplest way to enforce greater diversification, and hence tame your overconfidence, is to set portfolio limits. That is, you set a maximum percentage that you will ever hold in one stock.

Applying a portfolio limit recognises that some aspects of a company's future are simply unknowable. No matter how well you have researched a company, there are unpredictable events that can have a significant impact on the valuation of the business. Who foresaw that BP would have an oil well blowout that would cost them $62bn in damages and fines?[15] If this one unpredictable event could have this level of impact on one of the world's largest companies, think how similar events could completely wipe out smaller companies.

The purpose of setting portfolio limits is to limit the damage that such stock-specific unpredictable events can have on your long-term returns. Since you already know that you are overconfident, you should set portfolio limits well within the actual levels you think you are comfortable with. It is best to do this without *anchoring* on the make-up of your current portfolio. If your current largest position is 20%, for example, you are likely to set portfolio limits that are some way above that level to justify your existing portfolio to yourself. If you started with a blank sheet of paper, you would probably set portfolio limits that are some way below that level.

While the consequences may not be as severe as the total loss of value that can occur to an individual stock, the same principle applies in market sectors. Stocks in any given sector are likely to be correlated in their business performance, so setting a limit for the percentage that you will hold in any given sector is also a wise move. Holding 100 or more stocks that are all in the oil exploration sector is unlikely to be a sufficiently diversified portfolio. Even if you are an expert in the field and can generate a large amount of outperformance due to your investment skill, if the oil price falls significantly you will likely suffer large losses. In this case, taming your overconfidence will probably involve diversifying among market sectors or even asset classes. Adding passive exposure in sectors or asset classes where you don't have an investment edge is a good way of getting increased diversification at minimal cost

Personal Example – Toledo Mining

Early on in my investing career, I bought into a nickel mining company called Toledo Mining which had discovered a large amount of Limonite and Saprolite nickel ore in the Philippines. The company was operationally strong and able to quickly build a loading harbour to export the nickel ore via ship. From the direct shipping of nickel ore, the company generated significant cash flows which it was able to re-invest into expanding its operations. It had a long-term aim of building a processing plant in the Philippines to capture a greater part of the value chain.

Given the positive operational progress of the company and the extensive research I conducted, I allocated 10% of my portfolio to the company at an average of about £1 per share. At this time, China was desperate for resources to build out their national infrastructure and nickel ore was in demand for steel production. The market price for nickel ore rose, and with the Philippines ideally situated to ship ore to China, the company was producing as much as it could. The share price responded positively to these developments, rising to £5, making this 50% of my portfolio. Despite the high weighting, I didn't sell any meaningful amount because I erroneously believed that the rise of the share price was related to the operational success of the company. I had also run what I felt was a conservative Discounted Cash Flow valuation from the direct shipping of ore only and it came to £20/share. If they managed to develop a plant to capture more of the value chain, this would only increase further.

What I failed to realise was that it was the rise in the nickel price that had made the company so profitable, not operational success. Given the market dynamics, the nickel ore they were shipping was in demand above a specific nickel price. When the price of nickel fell below this level it became uneconomic to use this type of nickel ore, and no-one wanted it at *any* price. The company didn't have long-term supply contracts with Chinese smelters, so when the Global Financial Crisis hit in 2008 and demand for steel dropped, there was simply no demand for the direct shipping of the company's ore.

Combined with the poor general market sentiment for equities at this time, the share price of Toledo mining fell as low as 7p per share, a 97% loss from the share price high. I never sold any significant amount and held all the way down. The company did eventually recover somewhat and was sold for around 30p per share, but that didn't stop a 97% loss on a 50% portfolio position giving me a terrible investment year.

The only consolation was that it happened early in my investing (and professional) career, so the absolute size of the loss was relatively small. Through the experience, I learnt that I can't know everything about a company, and even if I did, there are external factors that can still cause me to lose. Most of all, though, I learnt to set portfolio limits.

At-Cost Portfolio Limits

In Chapter 5, 'Know Yourself', I broached the controversial subject of averaging down and concluded that it is a powerful tool in the investor's armoury if it is approached in the right way. However, it can also be a dangerous ally. If you get it wrong and keep averaging down on a company that generates a permanent loss of capital, either through bankruptcy or a failed business model that never recovers, you can lose significant amounts. This can happen even if you rigidly apply your portfolio limits.

For example, say you start with £1m in cash and you have set a portfolio limit of 10% in a single stock. An investment opportunity looks very promising so you invest £100k in that position. This investment then halves in value but still appears a very promising investment. Your portfolio is worth £950k so you invest a further £45k to bring yourself back up to £95k, which is your chosen 10% weighting. Suppose the price then halves in value again but still appears a very promising investment, so you invest a further £42.75k to bring your position back to 10% of your now £902.5k portfolio. The company then files for bankruptcy. Despite setting a strict 10% portfolio limit for any one investment and sticking to this rule, this investment has cost you £192.6k or 19% of your starting capital. You will have to generate a 24% return just to get back to your initial value.

If you think this example sounds unrealistic and you would never fall for this trap, then that may be your overconfidence talking. It has happened to some great investors with some great track records. Take, for example, Sequoia and their investment in Valeant Pharmaceuticals. Formed by

Bill Ruane and Richard Cunniff, Sequoia has been a value investment fund since 1970. It has serious pedigree: when Warren Buffett closed his partnership, he recommended investors move their money over to Ruane.[16] In the 45-year period from 1970 to 2015, the fund generated compound returns of 14.65% versus 10.93% for the S&P500. $10,000 invested in Sequoia in 1970 would have become $4.7m in 2015.

Sequoia invested early into Valeant and it was partly responsible for their strong returns up to 2015. Valeant Pharmaceuticals's revenue and earnings grew strongly due to their aggressive strategy of taking on debt to buy up orphan drugs and other drug companies. Valeant then raised drug prices and cut research spending to boost cash flow. Based on their growth rates, the company's share price reached a high of $265 per share in August 2015. As reports surfaced in October 2015 that Valeant may be using inappropriate sales channels to market their drugs, and the political environment started to sour to their price-hiking tactics, Sequoia had over 30% of its portfolio in Valeant.[17] In response to these reports, the Valeant share price started falling, halving in value to around $120 per share.

Despite still representing over 15% of the fund's assets, Bob Goldfarb, who managed the fund since Ruane's death in 2005, bought even more Valeant stock. Over the next six months, the Valeant stock price plummeted 87%, reaching as low as $33 per share in March 2016. Sequoia lost 22% of its value in this period and in 2016, Sequoia finally sold its shares in Valeant in the high $20s.[18]

The good news is that you can learn from the mistakes of these investors and leverage the power of averaging down to generate outsized returns when stocks recover, without undue downside when they fail. The key is to apply your portfolio limits to *both* the current market value *and* to your cost price.

So, in the example above if you started with a 10% position in a stock and your portfolio limit was 10% then you would not have bought anymore. The most you could have lost on a single stock is 10%.

Knowing that you have a limit to the overall capital that you can deploy into a single idea also gives you a greater sense of discipline. Instead of going immediately for 10%, you may start with an initial position of 5% so that you have the potential to buy more if the share price drops. The stock halves and you choose to buy another 2.5%. The stock halves again and you buy another 2.5%. At this point, with a portfolio limit of 10%, you cannot buy anymore. If the stock now goes to zero, the most you have lost is 10%. In fact, it may be slightly less, since your portfolio has probably dropped with the fall of the share price, so the two 2.5% purchases combined are less than the original 5% purchase. If the stock instead starts to rise, you have maximised your potential future returns by adding to the position at lower values.

Taking this even further, I prefer to set a lower *at-cost* maximum portfolio limit than my *mark-to-market* portfolio limits. For example, I may limit myself to investing 10% of my portfolio in a single stock *at-cost*. If the position rises significantly, I will only start selling for portfolio management reasons, i.e. to reduce single stock risk, at the 20% level. This has two advantages: the first is an extra level of protection against rapidly losing a large proportion of my portfolio from averaging down; secondly, it means I can maximise my *at-cost* exposure on the investment ideas that really do have significant potential, without immediately hitting a portfolio limit and having to sell some as soon as there is a small rise.

Leverage

Our tendency to be overconfident is also the reason that leverage should be used sparingly, if at all, by investors. The use of leverage places an external constraint on the timing of returns. For an unleveraged portfolio to go to zero it would require the failure of every portfolio constituent. While not impossible, this is extremely unlikely for a sufficiently diversified portfolio. The leveraged portfolio, however, could go to zero, not from complete corporate failure but from sentiment towards those portfolio constituents being sufficiently negative for a period of time. Leverage can enhance returns during the good times, but if an investor feels that it is necessary, then it should also increase their need for diversification. If possible, investors should seek leverage that does not have the right to be called in if the value of the underlying asset drops below the value of the debt. This may be achieved through the use of equity options, or at its simplest level, it may mean that an investor chooses to invest in equities prior to fully paying off the mortgage on their home. In both cases, a temporary decline in the value of their portfolio will not cause them to sell their investments, although it will increase their overall financial risk slightly, something that may not be a good thing for the already overconfident investor.

Thinking probabilistically

It's tough to make predictions, especially about the future.

Yogi Berra

While utilising higher levels of diversification than you think is necessary, setting portfolio limits and avoiding leverage can mitigate the negative impact of your overconfidence, there is another practice that can help overcome this: learning to think probabilistically.

In his study of expert judgement, Philip Tetlock found that most people made poor predictions about the future.[19] The expert forecasters in his research only did slightly better than chance and usually worse than simply extrapolating current trends. A particular type of person, however, made significantly better predictions than others: Tetlock called them *superforecasters*. Rather than focusing on narrow expertise in one area, as most experts do, superforecasters were able to gather evidence from a variety of sources and assess its likelihood. They worked well in teams, reviewed their own accuracy, were willing to admit error and were able to adapt their opinion. Having the superforecasters' probabilistic and adaptable approach will also help you temper your natural overconfidence.

Instead of simply thinking that an event will happen, or not, you choose to estimate *how* likely the event is, as well as listing the other potential outcomes and estimating how likely you believe they are too. This forces you to consider what may happen if the event doesn't happen and to plan accordingly. If the event is a positive outcome for your portfolio, such as a takeover, for example, your overconfidence means that you will probably overestimate the likelihood, but by pausing to consider all possible outcomes and avoiding making statements of certainty regarding future events, you force yourself to consider all the alternative scenarios.

Bayesian Probability

Bayes Theorem is a mathematical formula that enables you to calculate the chance of an event happening *given* that another event has occurred. (See Appendix B for details of the formula.) It is one of the most useful concepts in being able to think probabilistically. It reminds us to consider two things that are vitally important to creating good estimates of probability: base rates and false positive rates.

Base Rates

A *base rate* is the probability of an event happening independent of all other factors. If an event is rare, the probability of it occurring can remain low even if there are a significant number of events that increase its likelihood. Considering the base rate is what Tetlock calls *taking the outside view*: stepping back to see the full historical context in which similar events have occurred.

We are prone to forgetting about the base rate though, and unduly focussing on any new information that improves the chances of an event happening, thus overestimating its probability. This is often due to our use of the *representativeness heuristic*: the tendency to judge the likelihood of something by relying on its similarity to a parent population, or previous events.

As an example of how representativeness affects our judgement, consider the following scenario, again from Kahneman:

> An individual [from the US] has been described by a neighbour as follows: "Steve is very shy and withdrawn, invariably helpful but with little interest in people or in the world of reality. A meek and tidy soul, he has a need for order and structure, and a passion for detail". Is Steve more likely to be a librarian or a farmer?[20]

Given that the description of Steve is stereotypically that of a librarian, most people choose that occupation. Those that do, however, forget that there are more than twenty times the number of male farmers in the US than male librarians and that over 40% of adults describe themselves as 'shy'.[21] The base rate (of many more farmers than librarians) simply overwhelms the personality considerations.

In investing, the representativeness heuristic can lead us astray when we rely too much on the characteristics of our past winners to make future investment selections. Suppose the last few technology sector Initial Public Offerings have generated excellent returns for your portfolio. (An Initial Public Offering, or IPO, is when a company first lists on a stock exchange and makes shares available for the public to purchase.) In this case, the tendency could be to over-rate the chances of future IPOs doing well. Your recent experience means that you forget the base rate, which suggests that most IPOs make poor short-term investments after first listing.[22]

In addition to representativeness, the *availability heuristic* can also lead you to overweight the probability of events that are more easily recalled, such as those that have occurred more recently. If there has been a recent financial crisis, we are so attuned to the causes of that crisis we often miss the signs of the next one.

Availability bias may also take the form of how memorable a similar event is. We are far more likely to be scared of shark attacks than mosquito bites even though mosquitos kill more people in a day than sharks have in the last century. Being attacked by a shark is simply a more vivid mental picture, leading us to over-estimate the probability of it happening and fearing it far more than we should. Hence, when considering the likelihood of a particularly vivid market outcome, such as a very large single-day drop in the market index, you should always seek to find the historical statistics related to such events rather than relying on your memory, or the vivid accounts of others, to assess its likelihood, since you know these may lead you astray.

False Positives

To get a better understanding of the true likelihood of an event based on past indicators you also have to consider the role of false positives: how often an indicator flags something which turns out not to happen. False positive rates are particularly important in medicine. Suppose you create a very low-cost blood test which is certain to detect all cancers, but it also has a 1% false positive rate. This would appear to be an amazing breakthrough in the battle against cancer; why wouldn't you just test the whole UK population annually? Well, in 2015, 0.55% of the UK population was diagnosed with cancer.[23] This means that for every 1000 people, 5.5 people were diagnosed with the dreaded disease. In this example, our new test would have identified all of these people. However, due to its 1% false positive rate, it also would have identified 10 healthy people as having cancer. If your test came back positive you only had about a third chance of actually having cancer. Testing the whole population would put 650,000 people who turned out not to have the disease through a lot of unnecessary heartache and tests. It is for this reason that health interventions, such as general cancer screenings, tend to focus on higher-risk groups, such as those above a certain age, otherwise the false positives dwarf the real cases.

The same effect also impacts less life-and-death scenarios. Suppose there is a rumour in the paper that one of your holdings may be going to be taken over. You will want to assess how likely it is that the rumour is true. To apply this logic to give you the answer, (again see Appendix B for the application of the Bayes formula to this problem), you will need to know the base rate of how many takeovers occur in a given period, how many companies are subject to takeover rumours and, out of those who are subject to takeover rumours, what percentage actually result in a takeover.

Suppose 2% of companies receive a takeover in any given year, 5% have rumours in a newspaper, and out of the companies that receive a takeover, 50% first had a rumour in a newspaper. You want to know how likely is it that your holding will receive a takeover in the next year given that there is a rumour of it published in a newspaper. Well, out of 1000 companies, 20 are taken over each year, but only 10 of those are ones where the newspapers published a rumour first. 50 companies had a rumour published in a newspaper, including the 10 that were taken over, so the probability is 10 in 50 or 20%. Although much higher than the 1% chance that your holding receives a takeover offer without any rumour first, this may still be lower than you would intuitively expect without thinking probabilistically. The contributors to the low chances of a takeover are the low base rate (number of actual takeovers that occur in a year) and the high false positive rate (number of rumours that don't lead to a takeover).

Thinking more probabilistically won't entirely overcome your tendency to be overconfident but, by considering all outcomes and their likelihood, it may temper it somewhat. Well thought out *at-cost* and *mark-to-market* portfolio limits are still essential in your battle against overconfidence even when thinking probabilistically.

8
Overcoming Loss Aversion

We dislike taking losses; that alone is not surprising. What is surprising is *how much* we dislike them. We find taking a loss far more painful than the joy we get from gaining the same amount.

Imagine you are wagering on a single fair coin toss for an amount of money. If the coin lands heads then you have to pay that amount. If the coin lands tails then you win that amount multiplied by a factor. Since the coin toss is a fair one, then any factor greater than 1.00 would have a positive expectation and, from an expected return point of view, you should accept this bet.

Would you take this bet if the factor is 1.01?

Well, it turns out most people wouldn't. The reason is that losing money on the toss of a coin is just too painful for people to bear, even if they did so on a positive expectation bet. To get most people to accept this bet you have to increase the payout factor to at least 2 for smaller stakes, and much higher for bets featuring meaningful amounts of money.[1] Most people find taking a loss at least twice as painful as the joy of the equivalent gain. Knowing that we find taking a loss particularly painful, we go out of our way to avoid losses. This is what is known as loss aversion.

You can see loss aversion in action when you phrase questions about identical concepts differently. When offered a chance of winning a certain £100 or a 50% chance of winning £200, almost everyone prefers the guaranteed bet. However, reverse the question by supposing you are given £200 and then must either accept a certain £100 loss or a 50% chance of a £200 loss then most people prefer to take the gamble and hope they won't lose anything. Of course, the outcome is identical in either scenario.

We are risk-averse when it comes to making gains but become risk-seeking when identical scenarios are rephrased as losses. Our changed perception of the scenario, from one of gains to losses, is the only thing that has changed our behaviour.

Loss aversion means that we often take quite extreme steps to avoid suffering a definite loss even when it would be better for us to accept it. There are many examples of *Rogue Traders* who rack up enormous losses for their banks due to their inability to take a loss. Nick Leeson (in)famously brought down Barings Bank by hiding losing trades from his Singapore subsidiary in an 'errors and omissions account', rather than admit that these were trading losses to his superiors in London.[2] He hoped that he would make back the losses by selling insurance to clients in the form of options on the Japanese Nikkei index, in the expectation that the market wouldn't move too far and he would profit from receiving the premiums. When it did move against him, he sold more options, funding the losses with the premiums received. This, of course, compounded the problem. Following the market sell-off in response to the Kobe earthquake, these losses eventually became too large for the capital of the whole bank to bear.

Loss aversion doesn't just affect our financial transactions either: any perceived loss of reputation or exposure of wrongdoing can feel like a loss to us and we often take steps to avoid them. Some attempts to avoid taking a loss can be relatively harmless, such as forgetting to do a task at work and coming up with an excuse when a colleague asks about it. Some can have more profound consequences.

When Special Prosecutor Kenneth Starr found out that Bill Clinton was having an affair with a White House intern, Clinton could have gone on to national TV, admitted the wrongdoing, and begged for forgiveness from his family and the nation. That would be perceived by him as a definite loss, however, and being loss averse he was unwilling to do so. Instead, he rolled the dice and gambled that they didn't have the evidence and he could escape without taking this loss. It turned out he was wrong and he was almost impeached, not for the affair but for lying to Congress about his actions. Even though his conduct in the whole episode was less than exemplary, it was the actions driven by loss aversion that came closest to being his downfall.[3]

If professional traders and successful politicians all suffer from loss aversion, it is highly likely that you do too.

We often take steps to avoid taking a definite loss by simply not selling an investment. We manage to convince ourselves that it isn't a real loss until we've pressed the sell button. This inability to sell a losing position usually reveals itself in a portfolio by a long tail of very small positions.

These are the past losers: shares that we are unwilling to accept a loss on and sell. This is particularly illogical because once a shareholding is below a certain size, it has very little influence on the future returns of your portfolio. A 0.5% holding would have to double to have the same influence as the normal daily movements due to market noise of a 10% holding. If these really were our best ideas then we wouldn't be holding such small amounts of them, we would buy more and increase our portfolio weighting to one that reflects our view that the investment case is still a strong one. That these companies are still in our portfolios at such small sizes shows that we don't actually have much faith in them at all; it is merely our loss aversion that is preventing us from selling and redeploying our capital to more promising ideas.

The best way to avoid this tail of poor investments due to loss-aversion is to set a *lower limit* for the size of a position that you will hold in your portfolio. If the holding size drops below this level, and you are not willing to add to your position to bring the position size above this level, then you should sell.

The exact size of the lower limit will depend on how diversified a portfolio you have. It is unlikely that the same limits will work for someone with 15 stocks versus 50 stocks. Something like 5-10% of the size of your largest holding would typically make sense. So, if you set your upper portfolio limit at 10% then your lower limit should be 0.5 - 1.0%.

Although this is a straightforward rule to describe, it is surprising how hard it can be to obey this rule and sell those small losing positions.

When you face this situation yourself, and are struggling to sell, note just how powerful an effect loss aversion can be.

I can only think of two cases when it is worth holding a very small percentage of your portfolio in a company. The first is when the company has both an exceptionally high upside and a very large downside. Out-of-the-money options would come into this category, where the downside is a total loss but the upside represents multiples of the premium paid. It is worth noting, though, that most people over-value such lottery-like investments. If you have a portfolio with many of these types of investments, you should make sure you really do have an edge in these types of trades and are not merely lottery-seeking.

The second reason you may want to hold just a small amount in a company is when you want to incentivise yourself to understand it better. Many investors are better at really kicking the tyres of an investment proposition when they have some money on the line. These should not be indefinitely held positions, however. You should set yourself a deadline at which point you should have fully assessed the company prospects and either add to the position or sell it. The downside to this strategy is that *ownership bias* (see Chapter 12, 'Maintaining an Optimal Portfolio',) will probably make you rate the company more highly than you otherwise would. For this reason, this technique should be used sparingly.

Stop Losses

Another way that you can overcome loss aversion is by setting what are known as *stop-losses*. I mentioned these briefly in Chapter 5, 'Know Yourself', in the context of the research that Lee Freeman-Shor did into the traits of successful investors.[4] One type of successful investor, that Freeman-Shor calls *Assassins*, always utilise stop-losses.

A stop-loss is where you set an instruction, either automatically via a broker or manually via a set of written rules, to sell the position if the price drops below a set percentage of your purchase price. This can be an excellent tool for those who are particularly loss averse and for whom seeing the losing position in their portfolio causes particularly poor decision-making.

While some successful investors such as the *Assassins* find them invaluable, there are some reasons to think that employing a rigid stop-loss may not be always ideal:

- A stop-loss can mean you are making investment decisions based purely on subsequent price action from an arbitrary level (the price you bought at). The level you set your stop at, or the price you happened to buy at, have no fundamental reason for decision-making.

- Volatility due to market noise can cause the stop-loss to be triggered when nothing fundamental has changed about an investment. This is often referred to as being *whipsawed*, due to the shape of the share price graph that this effect creates.

- Traders or other investors know that it is common for people to place stop-loss orders at fixed percentages away from their buy price, or at round numbers such as £1.00. Those traders may profit from moving the share price of an illiquid stock in order to trigger the stop-losses of others.

- Using stop-losses is a widespread practice for *short sellers*: those who seek to benefit from the decline of a share price by borrowing and then selling the stock, hoping to buy back the stock at a lower price to return to the borrower. This is because there is no upper limit to a share price, so the short-seller has unlimited exposure to loss. The stop-loss is intended to mitigate this risk. For short selling, of course, the stop-loss represents a higher price at which the stock is repurchased rather than a lower price at which the stock is sold. For this reason, *short squeezes* can be common in heavily shorted stocks. This is where a price rise causes traders to close their position, and their stock buying causes the price to rise, triggering further stop-losses. In particularly illiquid stocks, with a large amount of stock lent for short selling, the short squeeze can take the share price many multiples higher, if often only briefly.

That said, using a stop-loss to sell and retain some capital is better than loss aversion preventing you from selling a company that really is about to fail. If you are an investor who utilises share price momentum as one of your investment criteria, a *trailing stop-loss* can be a useful tool, which is where you move your stop-loss to a higher level as the share price of your investment goes up. The idea is to capture as much of the increase of the share price as possible, but when the momentum starts to fade and the stock starts to decline you sell out.

Another way that may improve the positioning of a stop-loss is to take account of the normal volatility of the stock. Some businesses have more exposure to the economy or market conditions due to their product, industry, or level of gearing, and these stocks tend to move in price more in response to general market movements. Instead of using a fixed percentage as your stop-loss position, you would use a wider stop position for more volatile stocks and a narrower stop position for less volatile stocks. This way, movements in share price due to normal market volatility are less likely to stop-out the position unnecessarily. The aim would be that only unusually large share price movements, which may represent underlying changes in sentiment or fundamentals, would trigger the stop.

If you do decide to use stop-losses to overcome your loss aversion then it is clear that there is no 'one size fits all'; take the time to develop a strategy that reflects your unique investing style.

Whether you use a stop-loss or not, setting a lower portfolio limit, a level below which you sell losing investments that have become an insignificant proportion of your portfolio, is always a good idea.

9
Overcoming Optimism Bias

Most people are optimistic; overly so it seems. People consistently underestimate the likelihood of something bad happening to them. Even when presented with clear evidence that smoking can cause cancer, smokers often believe that they will not be among the ones affected.[1] It is the same for all manner of known health risks such as obesity, lack of exercise or sunburn. We are good at understanding the impact of our life choices in a statistical sense but have trouble thinking that we will ever be one of the negative cases. This is known as *optimism bias*. It is closely related to overconfidence discussed in Chapter 7, 'Overcoming Overconfidence'. Overconfidence can be thought of as a specific form of optimism bias regarding the things that are in our control, such as our own skills and abilities. Optimism bias goes further than this, though, and leads us to underestimate the likelihood of bad things happening even when we have no personal control or influence over those events.

Having an optimistic outlook in life is generally a good thing. Optimists tend to be healthier, more attractive, more successful and more resilient than their more pessimistic peers.[2] [3] With all these advantages in life, you almost certainly want to be an optimist. When it comes to investing, however, being optimistically-biased can have a downside: it means that you will likely underestimate the chance of something bad happening to the companies in your portfolio. You are also likely to overestimate the likelihood of a company's new product becoming a success. You will overestimate the potential size of the market for a product and underestimate the time and money that it will take to launch it. If you invest based on your overly-optimistic view of a company you are unlikely to make money.

Since being excessively optimistic is an unconscious bias, then relying on management to adjust your optimism by presenting an accurate picture is also flawed. Despite their greater insight, even honest company managements are likely to be over-optimistic about their company prospects. As investors, we often compound this error by optimistically interpreting the company's already optimistic announcements.

Unfortunately, it is very hard to overcome our tendency to view things optimistically, and it is not clear that we should want to completely overcome it either. Investment success is about the judicious bearing of risk, and if we are overly pessimistic, we may never choose to bear enough risk to make any real return. Dimson, Marsh and Staunton titled their book about the last century of global equity returns *Triumph of The Optimists* because those optimistic enough to invest in equities over that time have generated by far the highest rewards of any investors. In most cases, however, tempering our optimism with regard to individual companies or outcomes would improve our investment process and our returns.

Longboard Funds analysed the total lifetime returns of individual U.S. stocks from 1989 to 2015.[4] They found that 2,844 stocks generated more than 300% return, 7,928 generated between a 75% loss and 300% gain, and 3,683 lost more than 75% of their value. You may think the answer to investment success is to buy the stocks that generated 300% or more. While that would certainly be true, identifying them ahead of time has proved notoriously difficult for investors. The conclusion that Longboard came to is that it is better to 'play defence': to generate excess returns by trying to avoid the big losers rather than find the big winners.

Hedge fund manager David Rocker found that there were three types of businesses that generate almost total losses for investors: 'frauds, fads, and failures'.[5]

Blatant stock market frauds, where sales, resources or factories don't exist, often hit the headlines, but frauds can include any business that misrepresents itself or its earnings in some way. Some frauds are perpetrated by the unscrupulous, who out-right deceive investors, but many fraudulent managers started out with good intentions. Warren Buffett explains how the pressure to meet earnings expectations can start a company on this slippery slope:[6]

> What starts as an "innocent" fudge in order to not disappoint "the Street" – say, trade-loading at quarter-end, turning a blind eye to rising insurance losses, or drawing down a "cookie-jar" reserve – can become the first step toward full-fledged fraud. Playing with the numbers "just this once" may well be the CEO's intent;

it's seldom the end result. And if it's okay for the boss to cheat a little, it's easy for subordinates to rationalize similar behavior.

Like rogue traders, an inability to take a perceived loss sees management disappear down the rabbit hole of deeper and deeper deception.

Fads are companies whose product hits a wave of short-lived public buying, but investors make the mistake of valuing the current positive trend much too far into the future. Before too long the fickle buying public has moved onto the next craze, leaving the company with excess inventory and poor prospects.

Although not as memorable as frauds or fads, failures are the most common form of losing prospect. They are the companies that fail due to poor management, poor finances, poor execution or a combination of all three.

In this chapter, I go through each category of losers and identify practical ways that may help you to overcome your natural optimism and filter these out from your portfolio.

Avoiding Failures

While diversification is the only real protection against unknown unknowns, there are objective measures of the financial strength of a company that may help investors avoid failures. While the importance of financial strength is often well known to investors, they seem to have trouble using the tools available. Writing in the *Financial Times*, well-known fund manager Anthony Bolton notes:[7]

In analysing my worst mistakes over the years, I have identified three recurring factors. They are: poor balance sheets, poor business models and poor managements. Of these three, by far the most common cause of grief has been the poor balance sheet.

Given this, investors may be better off simply filtering out investments that may be at risk of failure using some of the metrics that help determine financial strength.

One of the most commonly used is the *current ratio*: the ratio of current assets (cash, inventories, receivables, etc.) to current liabilities (short-term debt, payables, etc.).

A current ratio of less than one may indicate a company that is having trouble meeting its short-term obligations. Generally, the higher the current ratio, the more able a company is to keep creating its products and paying its suppliers without being overly reliant on their banking facilities or supplier terms.

What represents a secure current ratio can vary from industry to industry. Retailers, for example, can trade successfully for years with negative working capital (and therefore a current ratio of less than 1) because they get paid by customers immediately and pay their suppliers on 90-day terms. In normal trading, the low current ratio of a retailer would not necessarily represent a distressed business. While their business is static or growing, this can be maintained indefinitely, but be aware of the impact if sales start falling. The unwinding of the negative working capital will cause negative cash flow at just the time the business is struggling. Sales declines for retailers with low current ratios are particularly ominous.

The other factor that may impact the current ratio is whether the debt is classified as a current or non-current liability. Accounting rules state that it will be a current liability if it is due in less than a year. Since the balance sheet presented in each set of results is just a snapshot in time, it may be that a current debt at the balance sheet date is now non-current debt following the renewal of a banking facility. Likewise, a non-current debt may start to become a current issue if it cannot easily be renewed in time. For this reason, it is worth looking into the details of the liabilities when a company has substantial debts.

In his book, *Choose Stocks Wisely*, accounting professor Paul W. Allen suggests that investors use an even more conservative approach to ensuring acceptable balance sheet strength.[8] His *Adjusted Current Ratio* is calculated by taking the sum of cash plus 80% of all other current assets on the balance sheet, and dividing by the total current liabilities. This ratio considers that, in a distressed situation, a company is unlikely to be able to realise the full value of its assets, apart from its cash.

Allen proposes that investors exclude companies with an adjusted current ratio below 1.2 from their investable universe. Although this may exclude some firms that are unlikely to face financial difficulties in the short term, this conservative approach may suit some investors better in their quest to overcome their natural optimism

In the example below, a current ratio of 1.32 would generally be an acceptable level of short-term financial strength for most businesses. However, the more conservative adjusted current ratio of 1.09 would not meet Allen's threshold of 1.2 for acceptable financial strength. The reason is that, in this example, a large amount of the current assets are inventory and receivables which may not be easily converted to cash in a distressed situation.

Calculating an Adjusted Current Ratio using Balance Sheet values

	2018 Accounts	Adjustment Factor	Adjusted Value
Current assets			
Inventories	17,643	80%	14,114
Trade and other receivables	22,106	80%	17,685
Cash and cash equivalents	7,646	100%	7,646
Total current assets	47,395		39,445
Current liabilities			
Trade and other payables	30,717	100%	30,717
Current tax liabilities	1,190	100%	1,190
Borrowings	4,132	100%	4,132
Total current liabilities	36,039		36,039
Current Ratio	**1.32**		**1.09**

Despite sometimes requiring a judgement call on an appropriate level of current ratio, if you assume that a company with a low current ratio, adjusted or not, is un-investable unless there is a clear reason why it is a special case, you will have taken a significant step in overcoming your overconfidence.

In addition to simple ratios such as the current ratio, there have been a number of models, created by finance academics, that aim to predict corporate failure and may be useful for the investor. The seminal study was published in 1968 by Edward Altman.[9] His *Z-score* puts multiple income and balance sheet entries together into a formula that identifies companies that are at risk of failure. Based on the output of Altman's formula, companies are sorted into three categories: *safe*, *grey zone*, or *distress zone*.

In the original study that used data from 66 manufacturing firms, Altman found that 72% of the companies that he identified as in the distress zone subsequently suffered corporate failure. It seems that, despite now being 50 years old, the power of the Z-score has not diminished: a follow-up study by Altman in 2000 found that the Z-score was still 80-90% accurate.[10] It does have some limitations, though, primarily that it is not suitable for assessing the strength of financial firms.

In 1974, Robert Merton realised that if he treated the equity of a company as an option on its assets, he could expand his work on options pricing to estimate when a company might be in default.[11] He called this *Distance-to-Default* (DD) and it represents when a firm's value may drop below the value of its debt and therefore be in default. The smaller the DD the closer to default a firm is likely to be. The benefit of his approach was that it was not dependent on the leverage ratio so could be applied to financial firms. Taking the lowest 10% of firms as measured by DD identified, out-of-sample, 65% of firms that defaulted in any given quarter.[12] The downsides of using Merton's DD are the need to estimate certain inputs and the complexity of the maths involved.

In 1980, James Ohlson created what he called the *O-Score*.[13] It updated the work of Altman to create a more accurate measure of the financial strength of a firm with a focus on simplicity and the added advantage of being represented as a probability value from 0-1, removing the need to remember threshold levels to categorise companies.

In 2011 Campbell, Hilscher and Szilagyi (CHS) created a model that has proven to be more accurate still.[14] This combined similar accounting metrics to Altman and Ohlson with some market data like Merton did. It also used probability technique called *Survival Analysis* to give a 0-1 probability measure, with the highest companies in the range 0.9-1 being in danger of failure.

Calculating these ratios for each investment opportunity would be a time-consuming proposition, but the good news is that a number of financial data providers include these as part of their company data sets. The cautious investor would be wise to simply filter out investments that show a significant risk of bankruptcy using as many of these measures for which they can access the data.

For those who don't have access to these tools, or want to be able to look deeper into the reasons why a company may be in financial distress, it is worth considering what goes into these formulae. There are certain common factors that they use to determine bankruptcy risk and it is worth going through why these might contribute to financial distress:

Debt (All metrics)

All of the metrics above use some form of measure of the indebtedness of a company compared with its assets. The higher the leverage, the less financial flexibility a company has; if it cannot pay its debts when they become due, it is insolvent.

Profitability (All metrics)

Being loss-making gives companies less time to be able to turn around their trading performance. Being increasingly loss-making over time suggests that any attempts at turn-around have not yet gained traction.

Liquidity (Z-score, O-Score, CHS)

Companies with larger amounts of cash, or higher current ratios, are more financially secure because they are more able to meet the immediate cash needs of the business.

Size (O-score, CHS)

Smaller companies may have fewer options for improving their financial flexibility by either rescheduling debt repayments or going to the market to raise additional equity.

Volatility (DD, CHS)

It seems that market price is actually predictive of financial difficulties. When the share price is volatile, particularly to the downside, it indicates that further trouble may be ahead.

I think most experienced investors would come up with a similar list if they were asked to think about what factors might suggest that a company was in financial distress. What is interesting is that these models use these factors cumulatively. A volatile share price alone would not indicate a company in financial distress, but when combined with high leverage and poor profitability, it may be a significant warning sign. The other thing to note is that despite these factors being well known, investors often discount their impact, presumably due to optimism bias. Having the cold, hard measure of the likelihood of financial difficulties, that these models give, can help overcome this.

Avoiding Fads

A fad is where a product or service captures the public's attention for a short period, generating high revenue growth that ultimately proves unsustainable. Investors often fail to separate the part of revenue growth that is driven by a fashion trend versus long-term secular shifts in consumer behaviour. This is hard to do without the benefit of hindsight. However, there are a couple of factors that may increase the risk of unsustainability in revenue growth:

- **Single product companies.** When the rapid sales increase is split across numerous products, a company is likely to be creating a brand that will have wider appeal and can be more easily maintained. Advertising by Burberry, for example, will potentially increase the sales of just Burberry products. Whereas advertising by Crocs may increase its sales, but it will also do so for those of similar foam shoes. Although Crocs does have some intellectual property protecting its products, that doesn't stop many similar products being sold in shops in every popular holiday destination that you will visit. When wearing foam shoes became unfashionable, Crocs didn't have a strong catalogue of other products to fall back on.

- **Products that are popular but not easily monetised.** These may be low margin products that have weak competitive moats, or could be caused investors buying into hype rather than reality.

In July 2016 Nintendo's share price doubled as the market cottoned on to the popularity of the Pokémon Go augmented reality game. The share price shortly gave up a significant proportion of its gains after Nintendo announced that it was the game developer, Niantic labs, who would receive the majority of the profits from the success of the game rather than Nintendo themselves.[15]

One of the challenges is that buying into a fad early can be very profitable. So perhaps the biggest lesson should be not to worry too much about avoiding fads completely, but if you are buying into a company that is profiting from fashionable trends, sell at the very first sign of trouble.

Avoiding Frauds

As well as causing us to underestimate the likelihood of financial difficulties besetting our investments, optimism bias also means that we may become a sucker for frauds. Financial fraud can take many forms, from companies who manipulate their earnings, to companies that make up their numbers completely.

Fraud can occur on any market. As Dan Davies points out in his book, *Lying for Money*, white collar frauds are actually more likely in high trust countries. An effect he calls the *Canadian Paradox* because Canada is an example of a high trust society which also has a reputation for financial sector fraud:

> It is much more difficult to be a fraudster in a society in which people only do business with relatives or where commerce is

based on family networks going back centuries. It is much easier to carry out a securities fraud in a market where dishonesty is the rare exception rather than the everyday rule.[16]

We can all fall for frauds. We cannot personally check every aspect of every investment. This means you must decide what to check, and every decision about what to check is also a decision about what you will take on trust. One of the issues is that investors place too much faith in a couple of things that they should probably be more sceptical about: accounts and accounting audits.

Investors often make an implicit assumption that the accounting figures they are presented with are fact. Although there are accounting standards that help to ensure that the numbers reported are, at least to some extent, consistent, accounting numbers are always based on management judgement and estimates.

There is some truth in the old joke:

> In a board meeting, the chairman of a company asks the board members 'what's two plus two?'. The CTO answers 'four plus or minus 0.01'; the HR director says, 'I don't know, but I'm glad we had this chat'; the CFO leans over to the CEO and whispers, 'how much do you want it to be?'

Some common judgements and estimates used to prepare company accounts include: when to make or release provisions, which depreciation methodology to use and what the useful life of assets are, discount rates for pensions, goodwill impairments and whether to recognise a debt as doubtful. There is nothing wrong with companies exercising judgement and making estimates, otherwise uncertainty would prevent companies from preparing *any* accounts. Companies are required by international accounting standards to report 'judgements management makes when applying its significant accounting policies, and that have the most significant effect on amounts that are recognised in the accounts'.[17] Investors would be wise to check that these judgements and estimates seem reasonable, especially if they have changed over time.

The second mistake that investors make is assuming that it is the auditor's job to detect frauds and that a clean audit removes all risk. The auditors are required to verify the numbers they can, but they will have a clearly defined audit scope and they will simply not be looking beyond this. For example, if a subsidiary company is audited separately, they will not re-check these figures on the ground but will accept the opinion of the separate auditor. We saw this with the number of Chinese companies that listed on US and UK stock exchanges that subsequently turned-out to not have the assets or revenue that they claimed to have. Investors were lulled into a false sense of security by the presence of a well-known auditor signing off the accounts. Since it was the separate Chinese subsidiary of the auditors that did the audit work on the ground, they were incentivised to agree to values they knew to be false, due to local pressures. The US or UK auditors took the values of the locally audited subsidiary accounts as gospel and audited the holding company without raising any concerns. In time, many investors learned to simply avoid foreign-domiciled companies that list on lightly-regulated Western exchanges to avoid the risk of this type of fraud.

Identifying frauds ahead of time is notoriously difficult for the simple reason that those committing the fraud are intent on deceiving everyone and will go to great lengths to do so. For this reason, investors tend to focus on what are often called *red flags*: warning signs that something may not be as it seems. Although one red flag may not indicate that something is amiss, the combination of many red flags raises the risk of fraud to a level at which you would not be prepared to invest. Not every foreign-domiciled company listed on a lightly-regulated Western exchange has something to hide, but it would be a red flag given the history of frauds occurring in other such companies. Taken in isolation, a single red flag may not stop you investing, but if it is combined with other red flags this should give you significant pause for thought.

There have been attempts to apply quantitative methods to the field of fraud detection. A commonly used tool is Benford's Law, which attempts to determine if published figures are simply made up.

Benford's Law

In a 1938 paper, Frank Benford found that numbers that are generated by natural processes, or from random events, follow a particular frequency distribution.[18] The leading digit of any number is most likely to be a one. The next most likely number for the leading digit is two, then three, through to nine. People are quite bad at making up genuinely random sequences of numbers. They often feel like odd or prime numbers, such as three or seven, are "more random" than even numbers. If accounting figures are made up, these numbers are used more frequently than the distribution of real figures would suggest. Likewise, people think that ending a number with zero makes them appear too exact and therefore more likely to be questioned, so they under-use zero as a trailing digit. Statistical tests can therefore be used to check that published accounting figures match Benford's law.

Of course, Benford's Law is now well known and clever fraudsters may use this knowledge to tailor their fabricated figures to pass these statistical tests. Although not foolproof, avoiding companies whose figures are flagged as high risk for fabrication under Benford's Law is a wise move.

The M-Score

Accounting Professor Messod Beneish came up with a measure of how likely a company was to be manipulating its earnings.[19] He called it the M-Score. It is based on a series of eight characteristics that may indicate earnings manipulation. Using a large data set of companies which were known to have manipulated their earnings, and those that had not, Beneish was able to compare the average values for the manipulators and the non-manipulators. Using statistical methods, he combined them into an equation that indicates if a company is likely to be a manipulator.

The precise threshold that is used to filter based on the M-Score depends on a compromise. If you filter too strictly you will falsely identify too many companies who are not manipulating, too loosely and you will miss potential manipulators. Beneish suggests a threshold of -1.78 as a good compromise, and many investment data providers give the M-Score for individual companies.

One way to use the M-Score in your investing decisions is to not invest in companies whose M-Score indicates they may be earnings manipulators. When seeking to identify earnings manipulation, I believe far more can be gained by understanding, not just the M-Score value, but *why* the M-Score uses the criteria that it does. In this way, you can look yourself for the characteristics that may indicate earnings manipulation rather than relying purely on a formula.

The M-Score formula adds up the weighted factors that Beneish found to be indicators of manipulation. In doing so, it acts as a red flag aggregator. If there was just one indicator of manipulation the required threshold is unlikely to be reached, but with several factors indicating potential manipulation, it is much more likely to be tipped over the threshold. Another advantage of understanding the M-Score more deeply is that occasionally a particularly large single factor may unfairly flag a company as an earning manipulator. This may be a unique feature of a particular company's business model, such as unusual working capital characteristics, and may not indicate earnings manipulation.

The first set of factors in Beneish's formula identify the type of companies that may be under pressure to resort to earnings manipulation. It looks for:

- **Reduced gross margin.** A reduction in gross margin suggests that the company is facing an increasingly competitive marketplace. Companies that face headwinds are more likely to resort to earnings manipulation to give the impression that they are still trading well.

- **High Sales Growth.** The rating of a high-growth company is reliant on showing consistently high sales and earnings growth. Given the likely severity of the market's reaction to growth beginning to falter, the temptation to resort to earning manipulation to continue to hit targets is high. (I expand on why high growth is an additional risk factor for fraud in the 'Other Red Flags' section below.)

- **Increasing Sales, General and Administrative Expenses.** A company that is increasing its SG&A costs may be having to invest more to generate its sales which may be negative for its future prospects. Again, short-term pressure to keep up appearances may lead to manipulation.

- **Increasing Financial Leverage.** Debt usually comes with covenants related to earnings and interest cover, to protect lenders. If covenants are breached this allows lenders to exercise much greater control over a business. If debt is increasing, a company may be more likely to manipulate earnings to meet these covenants.

The second set of factors in Beneish's formula try to identify the tricks management may have used to achieve earning manipulation:

- **Increasing receivables as a proportion of sales.** A disproportional increase in receivables means that customers are, on average, paying for goods later. This may mean that the company is extending better credit terms to customers in order to generate additional orders, or even choosing to book revenue from orders earlier than previously.

- **Decreasing rate of depreciation.** Depreciation is, of course, a cost to the income statement, reducing profits and earnings. If a company can change its depreciation method, or upwardly revises its estimates of the useful life of its assets, it will increase its near-term profits, (at the expense of profits later).

- **Excessive accruals.** Accruals represent one of the fundamental concepts of financial accounting: that revenue and costs are accounted for when the substance of the transaction occurs, not when the cash is received. Normally, this accounting practice gives a better view of the true performance of the business, but it is also open to abuse from more aggressive accounting practices. In the M-Score, accruals are defined as the difference between the operating income and the operating cash flow of a company. Cash flow failing to match earnings over the long term is one of the biggest indicators of earnings manipulation. Note that by using operating measures, Beneish's formula may miss some of the ways that management may seek to flatter their accounts; by capitalising development expenditure, for example. In general, shareholders should be wary of any company for whom cash flow is significantly less than earnings for extended periods.

As the Beneish M-Score shows, revenue recognition is often at the heart of many of these accounting manipulations. Beneish doesn't apply any sector-specific analysis, but it pays to consider the type of business a company conducts; some businesses simply have more leeway in their recognition of revenue. In a more traditional manufacturing business, it is clear when a product has been delivered. This doesn't stop an unscrupulous management team shipping products that a customer hasn't ordered and sending them an invoice that they know will never be paid, but the scope to undertake such activities is quite limited. When the product is intangible, such as software licenses, or represents multi-year contract deliverables, such as construction projects or software system implementations, it is much easier to increase revenue and profits by claiming that something was delivered a bit earlier than it was. I don't think it is a coincidence that some of the more recent allegations of poor revenue recognition by the UK Financial Reporting Council feature companies such as Carillion or Autonomy, which are in the support services or software sectors.[20][21]

For this reason, investors should pay particular attention to the balance sheet of such companies, since these manipulations will often show themselves in changes in the current assets. As already described, large increases in trade or other receivables can mean earlier invoicing practices. Such companies may also have large amounts of *accrued income* which is work they have done, or at least claim to have done, for clients but has not yet been invoiced. Large increases here are particularly concerning since this is where management can exercise the most judgement in accounting for sales. Likewise, if you see receivables or accrued income in the non-current assets this should raise questions since the company is telling you that they have delivered a product or service but are happy to wait over a year to be paid for it.

For those interested to learn more about the various ways that management can manipulate their earnings, then there are some excellent books on the topic, including classics such as *Financial Shenanigans* by Howard Schilit, or *Quality of Earnings* by Thornton O' Glove.[22][23]

Other Red Flags

High Growth

High growth is one of the factors in Beneish's test for earnings manipulators because companies growing quickly can often be under greater pressure to hit targets. In addition to this, Dan Davies argues that high growth is a further risk factor. If you want to continue to extract cash from an enterprise by fraudulent means, both the enterprise and the size of the fraud have to increase over time. The combined compound growth of both factors tends to lead to a snowball effect and unusually high growth rates. In his book, he proposes a golden rule:

> *Anything* which is growing unusually quickly needs to be checked out, and it needs to be checked out in a way that hasn't been checked before.[24]

Investors would do well to heed this rule. Davies' requirement to check out unusual growth in a *new* way is because, if a fraudulent company has managed to list on a stock exchange, it will have already managed to successfully circumvent the usual checks and balances designed to prevent fraud.

To check out suspect businesses, professional investors have been known to hire investigators in China to visit premises and check that they really do look like those of a multinational company. (They often found evidence that they don't.) While that level of confirmation may be out of reach for the average individual investor, calling up customers and suppliers, or doing a virtual drive-by on Google Maps certainly isn't, and may be very revealing. *The Sleuth Investor*, by Avner Mandelman, provides a good account of how investors may avoid frauds and gain an investment edge by doing on-the-ground research.[25]

Highly Acquisitive Companies

Although many legitimate listed companies use acquisitions as a way of successfully growing their business, acquisitions are also popular amongst fraudsters. The reason is that such corporate transactions provide a way of getting shareholders cash out of the company without creating false accounts.

One way this can work is that a fraudulent manager of a company gets a friend to set up a complimentary unlisted business. The company then trades with the new business giving the impression of a rapidly growing company that would achieve a high valuation. The company may even take a small equity stake in the new business, thus being able to regularly report on its success as an associate company. Eventually, the listed company makes an offer for all of the new business, paying a high valuation multiple. Payments may be in cash but can often take the form of shares in the listed company. Whereas a director would have to declare all sales of shares in the company, after a brief lock-up period the payment shares given to the "vendor" can be quietly sold in the market to raise cash. The vendor of the new business finds some way of sharing his new-found wealth with his old friend. Shareholders may actually be happy with the acquisition, at least in the short term, because it appears that the company has acquired a rapidly growing business in a complementary area. It can be years later when it becomes clear that the growth was illusory and the acquisition didn't live up to expectations. Unless the fraudsters happen to leave an incriminating paper trail, this type of fraud is very hard to prosecute, since all financial records will be technically accurate and look identical to those of a regular, if poor, business investment. It is only the intention to deceive that marks this out as fraudulent activity.

To avoid these frauds an investor needs to possess a high level of scepticism around acquisitive companies. Be especially sceptical of companies that make repeated acquisitions at high valuations. Look carefully at the management of the acquisition target, too. If there is a prior personal or professional relationship with the management of the acquiring company then all may not be what it seems. Such related-party transactions should be disclosed to investors, and when they are, these should be considered an additional red flag.

Previous Form

It is incredible how many fraudsters manage to commit multiple frauds and how many investors are willing to give them second chances. Summarising his research into frauds, Davies notes: [26]

> It's a sad fact, as my friends confirm, that if you want to find frauds, your best asset is a list of existing fraudsters. You might have noticed that comparatively few of the case studies we've looked at [in his book] were first offences. There's something about commercial fraudsters that keeps coming back to the same pattern of behaviour. And there's something about the modern economic system that keeps giving fraudsters second chances and putting people back into positions of responsibility when they've proved themselves dishonest.

As a society, it is important to give those who are genuinely reformed from criminal activity a second chance, but when it comes to your own portfolio, this is one risk you don't need to take. If any of a company's management has even been suspected of previous frauds this is a sign to stay well clear.

Unethical Business Models

There is a strange phenomenon where people know that someone is behaving unethically towards others, but they tell themselves that the fraudster would never defraud them.

There were suspicions circulating about Bernie Madoff prior to his investment performance being unmasked as little more than a pyramid scheme. What people suspected, however, was that he may be generating his exceptional results through insider trading or similar means and that therefore his reported returns were real. This is nonsensical, of course. If someone is willing to behave unethically towards other market participants, they most certainly are towards you too.

Dan Davies gives the example of Tony De Angelis, the 'Salad Oil King' who defrauded American Express, and others, by filling his storage tanks, that were meant to contain soybean oil, with mostly water.[27] (Oil floats on water so any cursory check on the tank would show the oil.) De Angelis actually encouraged rumours that he was in the New Jersey mafia, even though it appears to be untrue, so that lenders would think he had other sources of income which could back his debt. This didn't provide any protection to lenders when the collateral for their loans turned out to be sea water.

It is for this reason that I avoid companies that don't treat customers or other stakeholders fairly. In the past, this principle has prevented me from investing in companies that conduct activities such as: marketing scratch cards with premium rate phone numbers to claim the "prize"; providing subscription mobile ring-tones that are difficult to cancel; or persuading car accident victims to take high value cars instead of what they need, (sending the bill to the at-fault insurer, and by extension all of us, via our insurance premiums). The reason is that, if a company is willing to treat its customers like chumps, they won't think twice about treating shareholders the same. In all the cases these companies failed, due to either a change of regulation or poor management and I don't think this is a coincidence.

Obscurity

Avoid companies where you don't understand how they make their money or how they manage to be so profitable. Good, trustworthy management will be able to explain how they make their money, what their competitive advantage is and how that leads them to generate supra-normal profit margins. If a company is unwilling to divulge this information this should be a big red flag. Companies do have intellectual property that they will not reveal, preferring to protect it via secrecy rather than patent protection, but all should be able to explain the basics of how their technology works. If a company is reluctant to engage with their owners, they may be hiding something more than their intellectual property.

Changes of Accounting Policies or Auditors

Accounting policy choices do impact the reported earnings of companies. Changing the type of depreciation method, for example, may decrease the depreciation charge and increase earnings. Companies that change their policies for reasons other than adopting new accounting standards should be examined closely. Likewise, companies that change auditors frequently. It may be that an auditor is unhappy at the accounting policies a company has chosen but doesn't have the evidence or desire to qualify the audit, they may decide to resign quietly rather than upset clients or risk reputational damage.

Personal Example – Globo

Commenting on specific company accounting issues can be a minefield given that proving the intention to deceive is particularly difficult, and often this is the only thing that separates misrepresentation from poor business decisions. One company that admitted that there had been some form of misrepresentation, however, was Globo. On 26 October 2015 they released a UK Market Regulatory News Statement (RNS) that contained the following text:

> However, at the Board meeting, Costis Papadimitrakopoulos the CEO of the Group brought to the attention of the Board certain matters regarding the falsification of data and the misrepresentation of the Company's financial situation, and offered his resignation, as did Dimitris Gryparis the CFO of the Group.[28]

The RNS didn't detail the exact nature of misrepresentation or by whom it was made, but we can go through the reasons why I suspected that there were issues with the company statements prior to this announcement and was able to profit from their ultimate demise into administration less than two weeks after the above statement:[29]

- **Lack of free cash flow.** All the cash went on corporate transactions such as acquisitions, or in capitalising their significant internal development costs as intangible assets. See a summary of the cash flow statement below.

Globo Plc, Cashflow Statement, an extract, €m	2011	2012	2013	2014
Operating Cashflow	6.5	14.2	22.7	36.4
Net Tax & Finance Costs	1.3	0.9	1.5	4.7
Corporate Transactions	0.0	6.8	3.9	9.1
Purchase of Intangibles	14.5	11.7	16.0	24.4
Free Cashflow	**-9.3**	**-5.2**	**1.4**	**-1.8**

- **Large and increasing receivables.** A calculation of the average number of days revenue that the outstanding receivables represented shows that Globo was taking over 200 days to be paid on average. (See table below.) As a software company, Globo had significant leeway over its revenue recognition. They also had substantial non-current receivables, meaning they were booking revenue where they were expecting to be paid over 12 months later.

Globo Plc, Sales & Receivables, €m	2011	2012	2013	2014
Revenue	46.0	58.1	71.5	106.4
Current Receivables	25.5	22.4	31.3	55.0
Non-Current Receivables	0.1	9.7	8.3	6.0
Total Receivables	25.5	32.1	39.6	61.1
Days Sales Receivables	**202**	**202**	**202**	**209**

- **Suspect Cash Balances.** The company appeared to simultaneously hold both large cash and debt balances, causing what would appear to be completely unnecessary interest costs if the cash balance was real and unencumbered. (See table below.) The company regularly raised equity finance over these years even though it claimed it held significant cash balances. Finally, despite reporting over €100m of cash at the 2015 Half Year Results (the last results announcement prior to administration), the company was attempting to raise $180m of debt via a US bond offering paying a 10% coupon. A yield that suggested that the company's credit rating was effectively junk.

Globo Plc, Balance Sheet, an extract, €m	2011	2012	2013	2014	2015H1
Cash	9.3	19.2	64.2	82.8	104.4
Debt	8.5	5.0	21.4	42.4	56.9

- **Multiple acquisitions.** The company grew rapidly via acquisitions, conducting four acquisitions between 2011 and 2014, and had signed a letter of intent for a further acquisition when the company started to unravel. While there is no direct evidence that these acquisitions represent wrongdoing, you will recall that both rapid growth and acquisitions are well-known red flags.

- **Related-Party Transactions.** In December 2012 they conducted a related-party transaction that divested 51% of a subsidiary to its management and therefore de-consolidating the financial results of the subsidiary from those of the group. Payment terms for the divestment were generously extended over four years.

- **Changes of auditor.** The company's auditor, BDO, resigned in February 2014 due to an 'inability to agree a mutually acceptable audit scope in relation to our involvement in the work of component auditors needed to obtain sufficient evidence on which to base the audit opinion on the group financial statements'. Again, this resignation may have been for unrelated reasons, but the change of auditor represents an additional red flag.

As a final point, it is also worth noting the things that didn't make any difference to the outcome for shareholders of Globo:

- Unqualified accounting audit opinions.
- The actions of regulators.
- Investors meeting management or attending company presentations.

While Globo may be unique in how rapidly it fell apart following the announcement admitting misrepresentation, the same tools can be used to avoid stocks with similar risky characteristics.

Story Stocks

One of the reasons we may become suckers for frauds, fads or failures is our love of a good story. There is a multi-billion-dollar entertainment industry built on the premise that we will pay for good stories. While you may happily pay your Netflix or Amazon Prime subscription to be entertained, paying a high price for exciting stories is rarely a good idea in your investing practice.

One of the reasons we find stories so engaging is that our brains are hard-wired to respond to narratives. Consider the following short account:

> Sarah was overjoyed as the small aeroplane came into land, bumping along the barely maintained runway. The sight of the sun glistening off the clear azure sea and the smell of the fresh coastal air told her that the holiday of a lifetime had just begun. That the holiday costs were completely paid for by her recent successful investment in SciTek, made the experience even sweeter. The pain of the death of her mother, just three months ago, started to subside and a new chapter in her life had begun.

Although it's not going to win any prizes for literary fiction, when you read that scenario something will have happened in your brain that probably didn't happen when I described the factors that go into the Beneish M-Score. As I described the motion of the aeroplane, your motor cortex will have lit up.[30] The description of the sun and sea will cause your visual cortex to become engaged and your olfactory cortex will be stimulated by reading about the smell of the sea.[31] [32] Because more of your brain was activated, you are likely to retain any information in the story for longer. You will probably also be intrigued to know more about SciTek, despite it being a company I invented.

Since the character experienced familiar emotions, the joy of being on holiday and the pain of loss, the parts of your brain that feel empathy will also have been activated. Feeling empathy can cause the neurochemical oxytocin to be released and oxytocin gives a signal to the brain that 'it's safe to approach others'. The consequence of an oxytocin release is that you are more likely to trust the situation and the storyteller.[33] Emotional events also cause the hormone dopamine to be released which aids memory function and increases your enjoyment of the story.[34] [35]

You can see now why 'Story Stocks' can be so dangerous to our wealth. Our love of a good story can lead us to buy into the type of stocks that are unlikely to generate a positive return. Stocks that are loss-making, especially those that have negligible revenue, must have a good story attached to them because nobody puts up equity capital for an idea that sounds boring and unfeasible. Our emotional engagement with the story, imagining the returns we will generate and how we will spend the money, may cause us to trust company statements and managements far more than we should.

Our love of story stocks may also be due to some form of gambling instinct. We desire the excitement of betting on an unknown outcome, and where better to get tension and intrigue than from an investment with an exciting story attached? As John Maynard Keynes once noted:

> The game of professional investing is intolerably boring and over-exacting to anyone who is entirely exempt from the gambling instinct; whilst he who has it must pay to this propensity the appropriate toll.[36]

One way to avoid falling for story stocks, and paying the toll, would be to never invest in a company that has negative operating cash flow. Although this wouldn't be a foolproof method, it would filter out the stocks where you are most likely to fall for the fiction over the facts. You may miss out on some early-stage companies that go on to be big successes, but if an analysis of your past performance shows that you tend to be led astray by story stocks, this would be a good basic rule.

Another way to avoid getting carried away with the story is to follow legendary investor Irving Kahn's advice for reading Annual Reports and '...start at the back, where you tend to get the key financial information.'[37] By casting a sceptical eye over the numbers prior to reading any management commentary, you are better able to judge reality without being caught up in the narrative. If you examine the balance sheet and find that it is too weak to consider an investment you can choose not to read any further. It is incredible the number of times that a management commentary describing a strong balance sheet doesn't match up with what most investors would consider a strong balance sheet in the accounts. By reading the cash flow statement you get an idea of the true economic returns of the business, and if that cash appears to have been spent wisely, before reading about management's plans to spend future cash. If cash flow is negative then it will reveal how long the balance sheet can support such activities without returning to shareholders for further equity. By arming yourself with the numbers first, you can defend against the bias that a good story might cause, and better glean valuable information about the business from the management commentary.

The Narrative Fallacy

Not only are we unduly influenced by the stories we are told, but our need for stories is also so great that we often add in causal narratives that may not exist to events. This can affect not just the individual stocks we choose to invest in but the tools we use to assess the quality of businesses or managements.

The Harvard Business Review is full of case studies, on topics ranging from successful individual companies and leaders, to how to drive organisational change.[38] The problem is that the narrative of these studies is always added after the fact. We often think that successful business leaders or companies were destined to greatness because we only start to study them in detail after we know of their success. Knowing the outcome, we try to align aspects of the CEO's life history into an explanation of who they became. We may infer causality equally from early adversity *or* early success, from the unique opportunities they were afforded *or* the perseverance they developed due to lack of opportunity. Knowing that someone is successful, you can add a causal narrative after the fact to almost any life event. This is known as the *narrative fallacy*. The narrative explanation appears so strong that we forget to consider the multitudes of mediocre business leaders who had similar qualities or experiences and didn't stand out from the crowd.

In 2001 Jim Collins published a book called *Good to Great: Why Some Companies Make the Leap... and Others Don't*.[39] Collins used a large team of researchers and looked at more than 6000 articles and 2000 pages of interview transcripts to identify characteristics of companies that went from 'good to great', where greatness is defined by total shareholder return significantly higher than the market average over 15 years. He found seven characteristics that he believed explained their out-performance. The story was a powerful one because Good to Great went on to sell over four million copies.

The problem, as you may have guessed, is that looking for companies that have been successful and then poring over historical events in order to identify the characteristics that explain that success, is particularly prone to the narrative fallacy. Steven Levitt, the Chicago University economist and Freakonomics author, analysed what happened to the "great" companies post-2001. He found that this group of 11 companies actually *underperformed* the broad market going forward.[40]

The narrative fallacy affects not just popular business books but business school academic research too. Anyone who has any business education cannot fail to have studied Porter's *five forces*. Michael Porter's seminal 1980 work, *Competitive Strategy*, suggests that companies can gain a competitive advantage by analysing the interaction between five forces that shape industry structure: the bargaining power of suppliers, the bargaining power of buyers, the rivalry among existing firms, the threat of substitute products and the threat of new entrants. It is the role of manager to position their company to exploit the weaker forces and the aim of the investor to find companies that are able to do so.

Unfortunately, it turns out not to be true. All of the predictions made by Porter's model, such as a correlation between market share and profitability, appear to be false. In studies by Wharton Professor, Scott Armstrong, the application of Porter's five forces led to worse business decisions being made.[41] In his analysis of Porter's model, Thomas Powell, of Oxford University, concludes:

> There appears to be no falsifiable, unfalsified theory of competitive advantage, nor any competitive advantage

propositions defensible without resort to ideology, dogmatism, or faith.[42]

So before using such case studies or methodologies to try to find great business leaders or companies to invest in, it pays to seek empirical evidence that these methods add value. You may be as prone to falling for good stories in the research methods you choose as the companies you invest in.

This chapter has given you some practical tools to be able to filter out frauds, fads and failures from your portfolio. These methods will never be foolproof though: there will always be the odd disaster which was genuinely unpredictable. Consider the recent failure of UK-listed company Patisserie Valerie. In this case, it appears that some of the company management may have been using bank accounts that were not included in the published financial results and making many small false ledger entries.[43] This means that the published accounting figures did not give a true representation of the state of the business. Although all of the details have yet to emerge at the time of writing, it seems that there were almost no red flags that could have identified this ahead of time to investors. Based on the published results and management background, an investor probably would have concluded that the company was conservatively financed and well run. This is an example of why diversification is also an important tool to mitigate the impact of frauds, fads and failures.

Applying these concepts to identify companies which have a high risk of being a fraud, fad or failure is also likely to lead to some false positives. Sometimes you will mistakenly avoid companies that don't fail and go on to be excellent investments, but to use Buffett's baseball analogy: 'The stock market is a no-called-strike game. You don't have to swing at everything - you can wait for your pitch'.[44] There will be plenty more successful companies to invest in that do not possess these potentially risky characteristics. Given our tendency towards excessive optimism, it is far more likely that applying conservative assessment criteria will protect you from getting carried away by investment stories rather than miss great opportunities.

10
Overcoming Commitment Bias

The desire to appear consistent is a powerful psychological force. In his book *Influence: The Psychology of Persuasion*, Professor Robert Cialdini describes it as one of the six main ways we are influenced.[1] Cialdini is an academic psychology researcher at Arizona State University who realised the limitations of only doing research on university students in laboratory conditions. His genius was deducing that much more could be learnt from studying a group of people whose livelihoods depended on their ability to influence others: salespeople. In order to get greater insight into their ways, he replied to advertisements for sales trainees, became a used-car salesman and ran parties for multi-level marketing products. In all cases, he took these organisations' training manuals and his observations, and analysed them to understand which actions were successful in generating compliance, as well as the psychological reasons why.

All of the influential psychological forces that Cialdini found are effective because they are generally good ways to make decisions, or represent qualities we usually admire.

For the consistency effect, Cialdini states:

> To understand why consistency is so powerful a motive, it is important to recognize that, in most circumstances, consistency is valued and adaptive. Inconsistency is commonly thought to be an undesirable personality trait. The person whose beliefs, words, and deeds don't match may be seen as indecisive, confused, two-faced, or even mentally ill. On the other side, a high degree of consistency is normally associated with personal and intellectual strength. It is at the heart of logic, rationality, stability, and honesty.[2]

In one of the more insidious examples, Cialdini describes how the power of consistency was used to gain the compliance of American prisoners of war by the Chinese Army during the Korean War. The Chinese would start by asking a prisoner to agree to a simple statement such as 'America is not perfect'. Since the majority of prisoners would consider this to be a true statement, complying with this request wouldn't have seemed a big deal. Once they had agreed to the statement, however, the prisoners were asked to write a list of ways in which America is not perfect. Given that they had agreed with the statement 'America is not perfect', it became very hard not to comply with the second request and add some details: to refuse at this point would seem inconsistent with their first action. Once they had made a list of ways that America is not perfect, they were asked to read out their list on the camp radio, making the commitment public. A public commitment adds to the power of the effect since the number of people to whom you wish to retain the appearance of consistency increases. Compared to the harsh conditions of the North Korean prisoner of war camps, the Chinese camps were less physically abusive but far more effective at getting prisoner compliance. Breakouts were very rare and, given their public statements of compliance, prisoners often turned in fellow countrymen for minor rewards such as a small bag of rice. You can be sure that few of the prisoners understood where it would lead them when they were asked to agree with the simple statement, 'America is not perfect'.

Psychology researchers have since replicated this effect in a kinder setting.[3] In an experiment conducted in California, they approached households and asked if they would mind displaying a small sign on their lawn asking passing drivers to 'Drive Carefully'. Since careful driving in their neighbourhood was a public good and the signs were not particularly disruptive, it's not surprising most of those approached agreed to display the small sign. The power of consistency was tested two weeks later when the researchers returned to ask if the householders would mind displaying a much larger and uglier 'Drive Carefully' sign, that they had mocked up in a brochure. Over 50% of householders who had displayed the smaller sign agreed to display the larger sign, compared with less than 20% in the *control group* of householders who were not first approached to display the smaller sign. That's a significant change in average behaviour from such a small public commitment. We often make similar sub-optimal decisions when we are influenced by a prior decision that we want to appear consistent with.

These examples also show what is known as escalating commitment bias: a chain reaction, where we continue to make worse and worse decisions, each in response to a previous commitment we made.

When you understand the power of commitment bias you start to see its effect in many places. Ever wondered why, in order to enter the competition on the side of your cereal box as a child, you had to complete a statement such as 'I love [favourite cereal] because...'? It is not because kids are much better at coming up with advertising slogans than advertising professionals. It is because, by filling in the slogan, you are making a public statement about your love for [favourite cereal]. By making the public commitment, you change your identity from someone who likes the product to someone who loves it. You were more likely to keep buying that product in the future, or at least pestering your parents to buy it.

You can positively harness the power of public commitment when you want to make lifestyle changes such as doing more exercise or giving up smoking. By making a public commitment, such as signing up for a marathon and asking for sponsorship, you are much more likely to follow through with the training required. A personal tip: if you think you have a good idea for a book, tell all your friends you are writing a book. When six months later they ask you 'how is the book coming along?' you will suddenly feel the urge to get back to your writing room! If you are reading these words today it is at least partly due to the power of public commitment.

While commitment bias can be harnessed to make positive changes in life, when it comes to investing it can also have negative consequences. The investment prospects for any individual stock are complex and rapidly changing, so being fixed in your mindset or opinion is rarely a good thing. When accused of changing his mind on a TV program in 1970, economist Paul Samuelson replied:[4] 'Well when events change, I change my mind. What do you do?' However, as the accusation levelled against Samuelson shows, changing your mind when events change is surprisingly rare. This means that if you make a positive public statement about a stock it becomes very hard to change your mind and sell if the facts change. The desire to appear consistent overwhelms your rational decision-making.

The most worrying aspect about the desire to appear consistent is that we may be completely unaware of its influence on us. The same researchers who did the initial experiment with the 'Drive Carefully' sign repeated it, but instead of using the small sign as the initial influencing factor they asked residents to sign a petition agreeing with 'Keeping California Beautiful'.[5] Surprisingly this vague petition had almost the same effect as the small sign. It activated the residents' sense of civic duty and led them to accept the large 'Drive Carefully' sign in almost a similar proportion. Whereas some of the participants in the initial study may have thought 'hang on a minute, I'm only accepting this large sign because I accepted the small one two weeks ago', in this case, I would imagine very few people made the link between accepting the large sign and the petition they signed previously. Yet the evidence is that it was a significant influencing factor for many of them.

One way to overcome this could be to never make a public statement about an investee company. This would probably make you more effective at selling a stock when the investment case changes, but it may not make you completely immune to the effect. For example, I find this effect also manifests itself in the amount of research I do. The more research I conduct on a company, the more I want to appear consistent to myself that the hours of work are worth it, and the more likely I am to find justifications why the stock is a good buy.

Another downside of never making any public statement is that sharing research and investment ideas can be a crucial part of getting feedback and improving your investment skills. An investment life completely devoid of sensible debate would be an intolerably boring one.

In a recent interview, Charlie Munger attributes at least some of his phenomenal success to his ability to change his mind:

> Part of the reason I've been a little more successful than most people is I'm good at destroying my own best-loved ideas. I knew early in life that that would a useful knack and I've honed it all these years, so I'm pleased when I can destroy an idea that I've worked hard on over a long period of time. And most people aren't.[6]

So, what can we do to overcome our commitment bias and be better at changing our minds?

The simplest thing you can do is to build yourself an escape hatch: caveat your public statements with the reasons for your opinions. If those reasons don't turn out to be valid, you can take action without going against a public commitment you have made. For example, it is much better to say:

> If the company can reduce its costs to the industry average in the next year while maintaining current sales, the share price should be positively re-rated by several hundred per cent.

Rather than:

> The company is massively undervalued and should be several times the current price.

In the first statement you have given clear reasons why you believe a re-rating will occur. If costs do not reduce, or sales start to fall due to cost-cutting, you have given yourself a reason to sell. In the second statement you have simply identified yourself as a *bull* on the stock; an identity label that you may find hard to remove even if your potential reasons for being a *bull* turn out to be false. The first statement is also more conducive to generating quality debate. Discussions may centre around the ability of the company to cut costs and what impact that may have on the business. Although caveated statements are much better to avoid commitment bias and generate debate, they may not be as popular. People often prefer certainty to accuracy. This means your caveated statement may not be as popular on discussion boards or social media. Don't give in to the temptation to trade the ability to change your mind for social media *likes* though; in the long term, superior investment returns are worth far more to you and your family than a *trending* post.

Being able to make caveated statements about your investments can be enhanced by creating investment models. For those who utilise price action for their investment analysis, this may consist of writing down the positive attributes of the investment that currently cause you to hold it. For those who engage in a more fundamental analysis of accounting and business prospects, it often pays to have your own model of the company's recent past and future potential. The value isn't really in trying to predict the precise future outcome of company results. If the company's managers are not able to do this, you almost certainly won't be able to. The value in creating these models is in understanding the key drivers of revenue, profitability and cash flow, and then being able to assess actual results against these forecasts. This will allow you to identify where your assumptions may not be correct and take appropriate action.

Personal Example – Flybe

I initially invested in Flybe in 2014. Although this was a highly competitive industry, I believed that Flybe had some unique characteristics that meant that it had a sustainable competitive advantage. As a UK regional airline, it primarily flew turboprop aeroplanes on routes that were too short for a jet to compete with economically. Its main competitors on most of its routes were road and rail services. In the UK these options can be both slow and expensive, particularly at peak times. Flybe had a number of legacy issues, but with a market capitalisation below £90m, the company was both trading below net tangible assets and had the potential to generate significant future cash flows if they could reduce costs. They planned to achieve these cost-savings by handing back excess planes as their leases expired to reduce their fleet size. Although the short-term prospects were for further losses, the company had sufficient balance sheet strength to survive several years of continued losses without the need for additional capital. Given what I believed to be a strong investment case at the time, I made a number of positive public statements about the company on various forums.

Fast forward four years and the 2018 results, released in June of that year, showed that the balance sheet strength had deteriorated due to continued losses and, although net asset value was still £93m, net current liabilities exceeded net current assets. The balance sheet was unlikely to be able to support any further losses if they occurred.

The first quarter trading statement for 2018 was released in July of that year and showed that even though their revenue per seat (a key metric for airlines) was growing impressively, the costs were growing even faster. When I modelled the effect of similar trends on the full-year results, my analysis indicated the likelihood for further losses and cash outflows. Based on my model, with the reasons I invested in the company no longer valid, I sold my shares.

The interesting thing is that the market did not react negatively to the trading statement at first. If I had just read the headline numbers, I would have viewed the trading statement as a positive sign and remained invested. It would have been a costly error since a subsequent profit warning in October 2018 saw the shares lose 75% of their value.

Although there is clearly an element of luck in being able to exit the position without significant losses, it was having a good model of the factors that impact the business that enabled me to go against the initial market reaction and sell the shares. It could be argued that I should have seen the signs earlier, but it was the strength of my company model and my ability to clearly articulate my investment thesis that enabled me to eventually change my mind when the facts changed.

Following these events, the company put itself up for sale, unable to meet the ongoing cash requirements of the business as an independent

> entity. Given its then perilous state, the whole company was sold for just £2m; this represented only 2.5% of the value at which I sold my shares. Modelling the key company metrics saved me from a 97.5% loss on this investment.

So, next time you make a public statement about the investment merits of a particular share, it's worth thinking in advance of what events would cause you to change your mind and sell (or cover a short). Even better, write them down or create a model, so you have made a public commitment to yourself to change your mind if the facts change and you will at least want to appear consistent to that.

This brings us to the end of Part Two on behavioural biases. At this point, you should have a greater understanding of what they are, how they affect us and how difficult they are to overcome. You will be aware of the major behavioural biases that we all suffer from and be able to overcome your weaknesses by putting in place portfolio rules to mitigate the impact of those. In Part Three, I show how to bring it all together to build an optimal portfolio.

Part Three

An Optimal Portfolio

11
Creating an Optimal Portfolio

In Part One, I covered how you can play to your strengths. You will have learnt to focus your investment efforts where you have a competitive advantage, either buying smaller companies, special situations or by looking to exploit your ability to invest for longer than the average market participant. You will have ensured that your strategy fits your personality, giving you the grit to persevere through inevitable periods of underperformance. In Part Two, I described how behavioural biases can lead you astray and ways you can overcome these by setting rules for your portfolio. You will have decided what level of diversification is right for you, consciously erring on the side of greater diversification to overcome your tendency to be overconfident. You will have set both upper and lower portfolio limits and decided whether you should average down or not, and to what extent. You will have decided if a stop-loss policy is something that fits your investment strategy. You will also have understood where being optimistic might lead you astray and put in place a number of checks to avoid companies that are particularly high-risk of being frauds, fads or failures. Your portfolio will be enhanced by this process, but a key part of your investment process is still missing: portfolio construction. Your ability to pick winning stocks is important, but it will be your capacity to build these into a coherent portfolio that will really provide a secure financial future for you: one in which your returns have an acceptable volatility profile and where the mistakes you make, or the unpredictable random events you are exposed to, don't destroy all your stock-picking efforts. Good portfolio construction is vital, and at its heart is how you weight the stocks in your portfolio.

There are two simple portfolio weightings that are commonly used by investors: market capitalisation and equal weight. In addition to these, there is a more advanced methodology based on what is known as *Modern Portfolio Theory*. When used to construct real portfolios, all of these have some significant drawbacks. Before I introduce a better way, it is worth spending some time understanding how these popular ways of weighting a portfolio fall short.

Market Capitalisation Weighting

Most indexes are constructed using a market capitalisation weighting. If you buy an index tracker fund, you will be getting a market capitalisation weighted portfolio. This has several advantages. Firstly, if the overall market is defined as the combined value of all investible assets, it is, by definition, market capitalisation weighted. So, if you want broad exposure to all productive assets, it makes sense that your small slice of the investible universe should be weighted in proportion to all the available assets. Secondly, the market capitalisation weighted portfolio doesn't require rebalancing. Since the increase in price of any one asset within the portfolio increases both its desired weighting and its actual weighting equally, there is no action required to maintain the weighting.

Not having to trade to retain the desired weighting means that costs should be very low, and high costs are one of the big reasons that investors underperform the market. Most index funds will need to do a small amount of trading since companies enter and leave the index periodically, but the impact of this is usually small since, in the most popular index funds, such as the S&P500 or FTSE100 trackers, most trading occurs with the smallest holdings of the fund.

There are, however, a couple of reasons why market capitalisation weighting is not ideal. The first is that, by definition, a market capitalisation weighted index over-weights overvalued stocks and under-weights undervalued stocks. If a company is fundamentally overvalued its price will be higher than its true value. Since market capitalisation is a function of price, a higher price means its weighting is higher in the index. Conversely, if a company is fundamentally undervalued its price will be lower than its true value, which means its weighting is lower in the index.

This potential flaw with market capitalisation weighted indexes has led to the popularity of what is known as *fundamental indexing*: the idea that you weight stocks in an index by some non-price-dependent metric, such as sales or gross profits, in an attempt to remove the speculative market price from your weightings. Academic studies have shown that fundamental indexing may add up to 2% annually to index returns.[1] (Although fundamental indexing will add to your costs as this will need to be rebalanced periodically as share prices change.) Since, in practice, fundamental indexing doesn't look any different to adding a value tilt to your portfolio, some practitioners suggest that buying a market cap weighted value index is likely to achieve the same effect at a lower cost.[2]

The other concern with market-capitalisation weighting is that the largest companies in any index usually underperform, but this is where the index has the highest weighting. Rob Arnott analysed over six decades of global stock market data in a 2012 study entitled, *Too big to succeed,* and found that investing in the largest company in each market sector was a terrible strategy. Two-thirds of such companies underperformed their sector over the next ten years and the average return from investing in the largest companies in each sector would have been 4.30% a year less than the sector's average over that 10-year period.[3]

Interestingly this largest-is-worst effect also occurs in discretionary funds such as hedge funds. In his study of hedge fund stock-picking performance based on their published holdings, Meb Faber found that the manager's top pick is usually the worst performer out of their top 10 holdings.[4] If you want to build a hedge fund replication strategy you would almost certainly choose to exclude the largest-weighted pick. It seems that in most cases the position has become the largest holding due to price appreciation and not necessarily conviction. Hedge fund managers are too *slow* to rebalance their portfolios, on average.

Whilst index tracker investors accept these concerns with market-capitalisation-weighting in return for low cost and ease of execution, I don't see why a discretionary stock picker would want to base their strategy on market capitalisation given these drawbacks.

Equal Weighting

The second popular portfolio weighting is equal-weight. That is, you own the same amount of each of your picks. Some simple quant or income strategies use this methodology. The idea is usually one of strategic ignorance. You know that a set of stocks has specific characteristics that are likely to generate higher-than-average market returns based on some logical criteria or historical data analysis, but you do not know which stocks within that set are going to drive the returns. Hence you hold all the stocks that meet those criteria (or a sufficiently large sample of them) to get exposure to that expected outperformance.

While I applaud the equal-weight investor for their humility in accepting that they don't know everything about a given stock, I also think there are some logical reasons why this may be sub-optimal. By choosing to equal-weight their stocks, the investor is saying that they are unable to make any further assessment about the quality, risk or expected returns of each stock. They are very precise, however, about which stocks meet the criteria for inclusion in their set of investible stocks and which stocks don't. Such an investor is so clear about the criteria for including each stock in their investment portfolio but so unclear as to which stocks will generate the bulk of the returns. This seems paradoxical to me. If an investor can tilt their portfolio weighting towards those stocks that are more likely to generate higher returns, even slightly, this would add significant value.

Modern Portfolio Theory

Harry Markowitz came up with an elegant theory as to how you should weight assets in your portfolio: it was based on the rational assumption that investors would want to maximise the volatility-adjusted return that their portfolio generates.[5] For a given set of portfolio assets whose price moves independently, there will be a set of proportions of those assets that give an overall portfolio that maximises the volatility-adjusted return. Portfolios that achieve this maximisation are said to be on the *efficient frontier*.

When Markowitz created this theory in 1952 it was impossible to calculate the efficient frontier for any real number of assets due to the complexity of the mathematics involved. If you introduce an assumption of market efficiency, the market portfolio of all investable assets can be shown to be on the efficient frontier and we are back to using market capitalisation weighting. However, if you have read this far into a book about improving the portfolio construction of your stock picks, you are unlikely to be an adherent to the *Efficient Market Hypothesis*, at least in its stronger forms. With modern computing power, it is possible to optimise a portfolio so that it is on the efficient frontier, but there are a couple of reasons why you probably don't want to do so.

Like all mathematical models applied to the real world, they live or die on the assumptions you make. To apply Markowitz's method of optimisation you need to know the expected return, the expected volatility and the covariance of each asset, that is, the correlation of its price movements in relation to all the other assets. Practitioners often tend to take the historical values from the recent past as their estimates of these figures. The problem is that the true values of these are unknowable: you need to know the future values, not the past. If you are optimising a portfolio that consists of a stock market index and a bond market index then it may be reasonable to assume values related to the historical averages of these asset classes over the very long term. Even then, the correlation between major asset classes can change significantly over time and different economic conditions. For individual stocks, the volatility and co-variance are unlikely to be stable over even short periods. Likewise, while an individual investor may have an estimate of the level of undervaluation in a stock, they are unlikely to be able to predict when the market will close that valuation gap and therefore what the expected return of that stock is for a given time period.

While the theory may be of use to quant investors who build expected-return models of stocks based on known risk factors, the complexity of implementation combined with the uncertainty around the estimation of future values means that modern portfolio theory is not a good way of weighting the stocks in the average investor's portfolio. Perhaps most tellingly, when faced with the choice of how to invest for his own retirement, Markowitz didn't follow his theory and instead allocated it 50-50 between stocks and bonds, saying:

> ...I visualized my grief if the stock market went way up and I wasn't in it–or if it went way down and I was completely in it. My intention was to minimize my future regret. So I split my contributions 50/50 between bonds and equities.[6]

A Better Way

> Everything should be as simple as it can be but not simpler.
>
> Albert Einstein

I believe there is a better way of weighting stocks in your portfolio. One that is simple enough to be applied by the individual investor without requiring higher-level mathematics, whilst complex enough to improve on an equal-weight alternative. It is founded on the application of the principles of the Kelly Criterion introduced in Chapter 7, 'Overcoming Overconfidence'.

You will recall that John L. Kelly Jr. developed what is known as the Kelly Criterion as part of his research into the mathematics of betting games. The Kelly Criterion says that in a series of bets you will always end up with the highest return by betting the proportion of your bankroll in proportion to your edge versus the odds you are offered. (See Appendix A 'The Kelly Formula' for the mathematics behind these principles.)

The Kelly Criterion became well known when it was used by the legendary mathematician, physicist and investor Edward O. Thorp to size bets while using the card counting systems for Blackjack that he developed in Las Vegas casinos. Thorp published a best-selling book called *Beat the Dealer* which popularised his methods.[7] Each hand of Blackjack was an independent bet. Using Thorp's system, the card-counter's edge varied, from a slight advantage of 1%, up to 5% when the card deck was very favourable. When the house had an advantage, Thorp bet just $50 to keep his seat that the table. When the edge was 1% he bet $100, and when the deck was extremely favourable and his edge was 5%

he bet $500. In this case, there was no need to adjust for overconfidence since Thorp had accurately calculated his edge for the various states of the deck that he would come across and the odds of the game were known. The only adjustment required was to take account of the need to place small negative-expectation bets when the deck was unfavourable to keep the seat at the Blackjack table. The Kelly formula, of course, suggests that you shouldn't bet on any negative-expectation outcomes.

In investing we don't usually have a series of consecutive independent bets, we have a wide universe of potential investments, many of which may have a positive expectation in our analysis. Thorp and others went on to generalise the Kelly formula for portfolios of positive expectation investments. In his paper, *The Kelly Criterion in Blackjack, Sports Betting, and the Stock Market,* Thorp makes a rigorous argument for the use of what is known as *Fractional Kelly*: betting a reduced proportion, such as a half or third, of the proportion that the Kelly formula suggests. This is both to deal with issues of uncertainty with estimating the probabilities of outcomes in stock market investing, and the ability of investors to live with the volatility and drawdowns betting the Kelly amount causes. Thorp says:

> My experience has been that most cautious gamblers or investors who use Kelly find the frequency of substantial bankroll reduction to be uncomfortably large. We can see why now. To reduce this, they tend to prefer somewhat less than the full betting fraction f * [the Kelly proportion]. This also offers a margin of safety in case the betting situations are less favorable than believed. The penalty in reduced growth rate is not severe for moderate underbetting…

> ... Long term compounders ought to avoid using a greater fraction ("overbetting"). Therefore, to the extent that future probabilities are uncertain, long term compounders should further limit their investment fraction enough to prevent a significant risk of overbetting.

I would add a third reason for under-betting: our tendency to be overconfident and optimistic in estimating our edge and the odds of success.

Use of the Kelly formula became popular in value investing circles in the mid-2000s. Although there is no direct evidence that Buffett and Munger apply the Kelly formula directly, Mohnish Pabrai argues that they use the principles of Kelly regularly:[8]

> Betting heavily when the odds are overwhelmingly in your favor is something to which Warren Buffett and Charlie Munger have always subscribed. In November 1963, Mr. Buffett invested 40 percent of the Buffett Partnership's assets into a single business, American Express (Amex), where he had no control or say.

Pabrai goes on to describe how the Kelly formula may be applied to a former investment of his: Stewart Enterprises. This funeral home roll-up was saddled with a large amount of debt, but at $2 per share traded below its net tangible asset value of $4 per share. Pabrai reckoned that, even if the company entered *Chapter 11 Bankruptcy Protection*, assets could be sold to make the debt whole and equity holders would see at least $2 per share.

He estimated the odds of the following scenarios as:

Scenario	Chance	Value to equity holders
Selling funeral homes to repay debt.	25%	4$+ per share
Loan maturity extension	35%	4$+ per share
Loan refinancing with alternative lenders	20%	4$+ per share
Chapter 11 Bankruptcy	19%	$2 per share
Black Swan event	1%	$0 per share

He calculates that, with these odds, the Kelly formula indicates that you should bet 97% of your bankroll.

In his book, Pabrai also provides a good explanation for how to deal with the case where you have multiple suitable investments and how applying the Kelly formula, even fractionally, gives you an allocation greater than 100% in total: you would simply scale back your allocations keeping them in proportion to each other. For example, if you had 20 positive expectation investment ideas, and applying a fractional Kelly calculation suggested a 200% total allocation, then you would further halve your portfolio weights but keep the same proportions. If your Kelly calculation suggested that investment ideas one through ten should have a 15% allocation and ideas ten through twenty should have a 5% allocation, then your final portfolio allocations would be 7.5% and 2.5% respectively.

It is possible to conduct a detailed probabilistic analysis of the expected return of each potential investment idea you have, then use the Kelly formula to calculate the ideal proportion, and then adjust this down to a fractional amount, or so that the total portfolio allocation adds up to 100%. This is what Thorp does in his funds, where he focuses on option and other arbitrage strategies. By doing this, he has generated roughly 20% compound return, with just 6% volatility, over more than 30 years. This methodology is far too complicated for most investors to follow consistently, though. Tellingly it seems, Pabrai doesn't actually use the Kelly formula to size his positions:

> In my own portfolios at Pabrai Funds, I adjust for [uncertainty in estimates of probability] by simply placing bets at 10 percent of assets for each bet. It is suboptimal, but it takes care of the Bet 6 being superior to Bet 2 problem.

Although he applies the principle of Kelly to focus on low-risk, high-reward investments, he falls back to equal-weighting for his actual portfolio allocation, with all the associated drawbacks. This is still an improvement on most investors, who tend to forget about risk when they size positions in their portfolio. The common error is to get carried away by the potential upside of an investment opportunity and forget about the downside risk that is almost always also present. Pabrai deals with this by only ever investing in what he calls *Dhandho* investments: where the risk is very low and the potential rewards are high, where the Kelly criterion suggests that a large portfolio position is rational.

The problem with Pabrai's approach is that it leaves him holding large amounts of cash for significant periods, when he cannot find sufficient low-risk, high-reward opportunities. It seems likely that there are a number of positive expectation investment ideas that he passes on, simply because he won't allow the Kelly formula to guide him to hold smaller position sizes. Of course, holding a number of smaller positive-expectation positions doesn't preclude him from re-weighting his portfolio when the rarer *Dhandho* investments appear. Pabrai has used the principles of Kelly, Buffett and Munger to good effect, but given the low return on cash over the last decade, there is a reason to believe that he has not generated as high a return as he could have if he were more flexible on position-sizing.

I believe there is a good middle ground that is simple enough for all investors to follow but also applies the principles of the Kelly Criterion to create an approximately optimal portfolio. It involves assessing your investment opportunities based on the principles of the Kelly Criterion rather than the formula. First, let's explore those principles in a bit more detail:

Principle 1: Have a larger position size in stocks that have the greatest upside

Invest a greater amount in stocks that are more likely to generate a positive return or have a greater opportunity to generate larger positive returns. This principle applies whatever criteria you use to determine the upside potential. As a fundamental value investor, I tend to look at the gap between the current market value and my estimate of intrinsic value. If you are a momentum investor you may view the companies with the highest medium-term share price rise as the ones with the greatest upside. A quality investor may assess the quality of a company's moat and the size of the market that they can deploy incremental capital into. It doesn't matter what you use as your measure of upside potential as long as it is logical, estimable and consistently applied.

This principle sounds intuitively obvious, but many investors fail to adhere to it. This includes many sophisticated professional investors, such as the hedge fund managers in Faber's fund replication study whose largest holdings tended to be the companies that have done well in the past, not the ones that they consider to have the greatest upside today.

Principle 2: Have a smaller position size in riskier stocks

Holding more of the stocks that have the biggest upside seems intuitively obvious to most people. Fewer investors remember that managing the downside is equally important. This may be another consequence of our optimism bias.

The subject of what constitutes risk in investing is a hotly debated one. Finance academics define risk to be primarily related to the covariance of the share price movements with the price movements of the broad market. This is known as *beta,* and is the slope of the line-of-best-fit when you graph the returns of a stock with the returns of the broad market. A stock with a beta of 2 would tend to have exaggerated movements compared with the broad market: when the index is up by 1% the stock will tend, on average, to go up by 2%. The movements of a stock with a beta of 0.5 would be dampened compared with the broad market: when the index is up by 1% the stock will tend, on average, to go up by just 0.5%.

There is some logic to volatility being a measure of risk; volatility does matter to investors, particularly, as discussed in Chapter 3, 'Think Long Term', for professional money managers who bear career or redemption risk during periods of low returns. The individual investor can suffer from volatility "risk" too by having to explain to a spouse why they are going to Blackpool on holiday this year not Barbados! As I covered in Chapter 8, 'Overcoming Loss Aversion', there is also a high likelihood that severe price declines would cause an investor to behave illogically.

One of the standard measures of risk-adjusted returns is the Sharpe ratio. This is calculated by taking the excess return above the risk-free rate (usually taken to be the interest rate on short-term government bonds) and dividing by the annualised volatility. Over the long term, UK equities have had a Sharpe ratio of 0.33.[9] The theory is that only volatility-adjusted returns represent true outperformance. If your outperformance comes at the cost of even greater volatility, you could get the better returns with the same volatility by simply gearing up your exposure to the broad index. The theory also says that you would prefer an investment strategy that had excess returns of 3% and an annualised volatility of 1% (and therefore a Sharpe ratio of 3) to owning the broad market index that has historically had excess returns of around 10% over the long term (but a Sharpe ratio of 0.33). The theory is that you could gear up the investment strategy to generate the same returns as the broad stock market and still have lower volatility of returns.

In reality, it is unlikely that an individual investor could gear up their strategy at the risk-free rate (since you are unlikely to be viewed as credit-worthy as a government that can print its own currency). It is real returns, not risk-adjusted returns, that pay the bills. So, while the Sharpe ratio is a good tool to check that those to whom you entrust your money are generating true outperformance, when managing your own portfolio you should aim for the maximum return you can get, as long as it doesn't come at the cost of a volatility level that would cause you to make poor investment decisions.

Whilst I agree that volatility does represent risk, it would seem naïve to consider it the only form of risk an investor is exposed to. By investing in a strategy with a historically high Sharpe ratio you may be merely swapping volatility for *tail risk*, that is, taking on exposure to very negative but rare events. An example of this would be *put option* selling strategies. The seller of a put option is giving the option to the buyer to sell a stock or index to them at a predetermined *strike price*, in return for a small premium. Of course, the buyer of the put option is only going to exercise their option when the price of the underlying asset has dropped below that of the option strike price so that being able to sell at a higher price is profitable. In a rising market, a put-option selling strategy would receive a small premium each month, and with no losses, would appear to have a high Sharpe ratio. On the day the market crashes the strategy will generate large losses, often more than all the previous gains. It is also worth noting that Bernie Madoff had a very high Sharpe ratio prior to his investment fund being exposed as a pyramid scheme. If you are going to make the numbers up then you might as well make them up consistently. Of course, in these examples, the high Sharpe ratio has told you nothing about the level of risk you are bearing.

Another common definition of investment risk is that it is the chance of a permanent loss of capital, which again is true, but difficult to apply in a portfolio management context. For every investment, there is a set of events that is so extreme that it can lead to a total loss, and most investors are bad at assessing the probabilities of extreme events. They just don't happen often enough for us to get enough data to judge them accurately. We need to be able to approximately assess the risk of a stock in a way that doesn't require us to analyse extreme events.

Therefore, in addition to volatility, I can see at least eight distinct forms of risk an investor should be aware of in assessing the risk level of a current or potential investment:

Financing Risk - Companies with high levels of debt, or weak balance sheets, will be less able to weather a period of poor trading. A heavily loss-making company, or one with large cash outflows, may struggle to raise extra capital. The same tools discussed in Chapter 9, 'Overcoming Optimism Bias', such as the *Current Ratio* or the *Altman Z-Score*, can be used to assess the financial strength of the company. The focus in Chapter 9 was on completely avoiding the worst stocks with a significant risk of financial problems in the near future. The focus here is assessing the overall financial strength of a company, that isn't at immediate risk of financial distress, to determine its longer-term risk profile.

Management Risk - Management with a history of poor capital allocation, or being overly promotional, will add an additional risk factor. Ideally, you want company management with a history of making conservative commitments and consistently hitting these. Although an overly smooth earnings profile may indicate that the management is engaged in earnings manipulation, in general, consistency of performance is a good thing. In his book, *The Outsiders*, William Thorndike analyses eight CEOs who were great capital allocators and had delivered tremendous returns for shareholders.[10] He found that they all shared certain characteristics: they followed a highly decentralised approach when it came to operational management but a highly centralised one when it came to capital allocation decisions; they tended to buy back shares when they are historically cheap and issue shares for acquisitions when they are at elevated levels; and their main measure of corporate success was after-tax cash flow returns. Even though such management may appear to be less engaged with shareholders than the average company, they should be considered a safe pair of hands. A management that takes the opposite tack: being overly controlling, empire-building at any cost, or focusing on obscure performance metrics, should be considered high-risk, whatever they espouse about shareholder value in their frequent corporate presentations.

In addition, the more closely aligned management incentives are to shareholders the lower risk a company is likely to be. Ideally, company management will also be significant shareholders and their stake in the company will be many multiples of their salary, but not enough so that they control the company. Where the management team are offered share options, these should be tied to demanding operational performance targets and issued at a premium to the current share price. Conversely, the presence of *related party transactions*, where the company trades with or buys other companies or assets that are controlled by the management, increases the risk to shareholders. It is possible that these transactions may not be undertaken solely in the interests of all shareholders. The standard way of dealing with conflicts of interest is through disclosure, but in reality, this is often insufficient to overcome the problem. In one study by Daylian Cain, George

Loewenstein and Don Moore, when a conflict of interest was disclosed, those receiving the disclosure did adapt their view to take into account the conflict of interest.[11] By making the disclosure, however, the disclosers in the study felt justified in adapting their position *even more* favourably to themselves. The net result was that the disclosure did not neutralise the conflict of interest and may have made it worse. The same effect likely applies to related party transactions.

Product Risk - Companies with one product or a few products, serving only one market, are more exposed to the performance of that product or market. Likewise, a company that sells a high percentage of its products to a single customer is higher risk than one that has many customers. Typically, but not exclusively, this makes smaller companies riskier.

Liquidity Risk - The risk of not being able to sell near the published market price when you want to. Again, this usually makes smaller companies riskier.

Commodity Risk - Companies without a sustainable competitive advantage to control pricing are more likely to be exposed to commodity pricing, economic growth, inflation or obsolescence factors. Companies that operate with low margins may still be good investments if they excel operationally, but low margins do increase the risk that any downturn will push the company into a loss-making position.

Correlation Risk - By correlation, I don't mean the mathematical co-variance of share prices but the common exposure they have to economic factors that are out of your control. For example, if you already have an oil explorer in your portfolio adding a second one should be considered higher risk (all other things being equal), than adding an equally undervalued oil consumer, such as a plastics manufacturer.

Regulatory Risk - Some companies generate profits because they are adept at navigating a regulatory environment. For example, a company may have particular expertise in achieving planning permission for its property developments. The risk is that changes of government or public opinion will cause the regulations to change to the detriment of the company.

Another type of regulatory risk that companies face is when their products are deemed to be damaging to society; these activities may be banned altogether by new regulations. As discussed in Chapter 9, 'Overcoming Optimism Bias', it is my belief and experience that these sorts of companies are best avoided whatever the superficial attraction. With this type of company, it is not just the regulatory risk that one faces but that if management doesn't mind damaging the well-being of their customers, they are unlikely to worry about damaging the wallet of their shareholders.

Country or Political Risk - The quality of protections for companies or investors varies significantly across the world. Organisations such as Transparency International publish rankings for countries on measures such as corruption.[12] Companies who have significant operations in countries that are low on these scales should be considered high risk whatever the other investment attributes.

While different investments will have very different characteristics, this is one area where it is best to be approximately right rather than precisely wrong. When viewed objectively, most investors can broadly categorise the risk level of their holdings with ease. We all intuitively understand that a company with a single exploration mining asset or one who operates solely in countries where corruption is widespread are high-risk investments. Equally, it is easy to understand that companies with strong balance sheets, diversified operations across stable countries, and recurring revenue from multiple customers are low risk. While it pays to go through all the potential types of risk and assess them for each company you analyse, the biggest mistake investors make is getting carried away with the upside potential of a high-risk investment and ending up with too large a position size when they know the investment is high risk.

It is not the analysis of risk that leads most investors astray but the disciplined application of the principle of the Kelly Criterion which says to reduce position size as risk increases. For this reason, I suggest dispensing with any complex assessment criteria and settling on something simple, such as a low-medium-high risk categorisation.

Applying the Principles

The key to good portfolio construction is to apply both of the Kelly principles simultaneously to determine your position-sizing. You create a matrix where your position size is determined by your categorisation of the upside potential *and* the downside risk. Your largest positions, of course, should be the ones where you consider the upside to be large and the chance of negative outcomes to be low, or the consequences of negative outcomes to be minimal.

Overall, with three categories, low, medium and high, for assessing both risk and reward, your allocation strategy would look something similar to this:

Ideal Position Size		Reward (Potential Upside)		
^^	^^	Low	Medium	High
Risk (Potential Downside)	Low		Medium	Large
^^	Medium		Small	Medium
^^	High			Small

(Note: For readability, throughout this section, blank cells represent zero weighting).

For low-risk investments with a good return potential, or slightly riskier stocks with an excellent expected return, you can allocate a reasonable amount of your portfolio to them, just not as much as you would for the low-risk, high-reward investments. If you find stocks that have a high potential return but are also risky you should invest, but limit yourself to small positions in these types of opportunities. These could include options strategies if you are sufficiently familiar with such instruments. If such investments pay off, the returns will be high even from very modest positions. Finally, you would choose to hold no investments which have low expected returns, whatever their risk level. This also means that you choose to sell investments when your analysis indicates that they no longer have any significant upside.

It is owning these medium and small positions that differentiate this strategy from that of Mohnish Pabrai, who chooses to own only the large low-risk, high-reward positions. Pabrai's strategy has the downside that

CREATING AN OPTIMAL PORTFOLIO

he often holds very large amounts of cash and hence has significant return volatility due to only holding concentrated positions.

The precise percentage values you choose will vary depending on your optimal level of diversification and the availability of good investment ideas that meet your criteria. When you have an abundance of ideas that meet your investment criteria, scale back your percentage allocations to get back to 100%, in the same way that Pabrai scales back his positions.

For example, suppose you work out your ideal position size to be as follows:

Ideal Position Size		Reward (Potential Upside)		
^^	^^	Low	Medium	High
Risk (Potential Downside)	Low		5%	10%
^^	Medium		2%	5%
^^	High			2%

However, in current market conditions, you are finding an abundance of good opportunities:

Number of investment ideas		Reward (Potential Upside)		
^^	^^	Low	Medium	High
Risk (Potential Downside)	Low		10	7
^^	Medium		4	12
^^	High			6

If you applied your ideal position sizes you would end up with a 200% allocation. In this case, you would scale back your ideal position size by a factor of 2:

Actual Position Size		Reward (Potential Upside)		
		Low	Medium	High
Risk (Potential Downside)	Low		2.5%	5%
	Medium		1%	2.5%
	High			1%

Applied correctly, and assuming you are able to approximately judge the risk and reward factors correctly at least some of the time, the risk-reward weighted portfolio should beat every other form of portfolio weighting. This is what Kelly proved with his mathematical treatment of these concepts.

How Much Cash Should You Hold?

The average individual investor holds quite a lot of cash. The American Association of Individual Investors (AAII) Asset Allocation Survey puts the average at 23%, for US-based investors, over the last 30 years.[13] Given that the average equity fund held just 3.5% in cash, and both equities and bonds have outperformed cash over most long periods, investment writer Cullen Roche makes the argument that this is one of the main reasons that individual investors underperform their professional equivalents.[14]

Of course, a sensible investor will have cash holdings for any short and medium-term expenses and will only invest in the stock market for their long-term savings. The AAII survey is asking about investors' dealing accounts though, so this is typically cash allocated for long-term investments, not short-term needs.

So why do individual investors tend to hold so much cash?

Investment strategist Samuel Lee says:

> In my experience, investors sitting on a lot of cash are usually worried about equity valuations or the economy, and tell themselves and others that they are going to buy gobs of stock *after* a crash. The strategy sounds prudent and has common sense appeal – everyone knows that one should be fearful when others are greedy, greedy when others are fearful.[15]

Roche suggests that holding large amounts of cash is due to short-term thinking, with investors overvaluing the certainty of large cash holdings. When you ask investors why they hold cash it is usually to take advantage of market weakness. We feel clever when the market sells off and we are holding a lot of cash, and dumb when we are fully invested. While the aim is laudable, we pay a high price for feeling smart.

Lee simulated a simple strategy of buying the stock market index on varying levels of weakness, and then selling once the market had returned to the level prior to the drop, or after different periods: one, three or five years. Using US market data from 1926-2016 and drawdown thresholds of -10% through to -50%, Lee found that every single combination of drawdown threshold and holding period generated poorer returns, both on an absolute basis and a volatility-adjusted one, than a simple buy-and-hold strategy. The best of the *buy-the-dip* strategies was to buy on a 45% drawdown and hold for five years, but even this had a *Sharpe Ratio* (a measure of return per unit of volatility) of 0.26 compared with a Sharpe Ratio of 0.34 for a buy and hold strategy over the same period.

This buy-the-dip strategy doesn't work because historically the equity risk premium has been high, waiting for a 45% drawdown requires years of sitting in cash and because the market tends to exhibit momentum not mean reversion over these sort of time periods.

If mechanical buy-the-dip strategies don't work, maybe investors can use their experience to determine when to hold large amounts of cash and when to be fully invested?

The problem with this idea is that the average individual investor is very bad at calling the short-term direction of the market. To see this, you only have to look at the difference between the average returns of stock market funds and the weighted average returns of investors in those funds. These sound like the same concept but are subtly different: the first is the return if all investors had simply bought and held the fund, the latter is the return when you take into account trading in and out of the fund by investors. On average, investors' attempts at timing *cost* them 0.81% per year in lost returns. It doesn't sound much but compounds up to a 26% underperformance over a 30-year investment timeframe.[16] The situation is likely to be even worse in more volatile investment funds. For example, consider the investors in the CGM Focus Fund run by Ken Heebner. According to Morningstar, Heebner was the best performing fund manager for the decade ending 2009, delivering 18% compound annual return during this time. The average investor in the fund, however, generated an 11% compound annual *loss* during the same period.[17] They created this massive 29% annual underperformance for themselves by buying into the fund after it had posted strong returns and bailing after it suffered losses.

Investors tend to spot too many crises and sell up too often, a problem originating from our history as hunter-gatherers. If you spotted an imaginary tiger in the jungle and ran away, the consequence was a bit of unnecessary spent energy. If you failed to spot a real tiger, the consequence would be much more severe. Those who were bad at spotting and reacting to danger didn't last long enough to have much impact on the gene pool. Today, we tend to see tigers in the market far more often than they actually appear.

We then compound this error by succumbing to fear during actual market corrections and failing to buy back on market weakness. A number of shrewd investors spotted the 2008 financial crisis, realised its severity, and sold all their equities. There is a much smaller number, however, who then spotted that the market was historically cheap in the spring of 2009 and reinvested. Many missed the early rises and never got back in, waiting for the market to return to lows that never came. Given the strong stock market performance over the following decade, and that cash has paid virtually zero interest in this time, even these most prescient of investors may have been better off simply remaining fully invested.

I think the only time that you should hold a significant proportion of cash is when you cannot find enough investments with acceptable risk-reward characteristics and your portfolio limits prevent you from being fully invested.

For example, suppose you had the same ideal risk-reward matrix as the previous example:

Ideal Position Size		Reward (Potential Upside)		
		Low	Medium	High
Risk (Potential Downside)	Low		5%	10%
	Medium		2%	5%
	High			2%

Suppose also that you have set an *at-cost* portfolio limit for yourself (the amount you are willing to invest in a single stock) of 10% and have only managed to identify nine investment ideas split amongst the following categories:

Number of investment ideas		Reward (Potential Upside)		
		Low	Medium	High
Risk (Potential Downside)	Low		2	3
	Medium		2	1
	High			1

You would hold only nine stocks because you could only identify nine opportunities for investment that met your criteria. These would represent 51% (calculated from: 3 x 10% + 3 x 5% + 3 x 2%) of your portfolio. In this case, you would also hold 49% cash, which provides the protection against unknown unknowns that would normally be provided by holding a more diversified portfolio and allows you to invest when new investment opportunities arise.

Although holding large amounts of cash when you have sufficient investment ideas to deploy your capital is unwise, this doesn't mean that the general stock market *indices* are always a buy. Howard Marks talks about the importance of knowing the economic cycle and having an idea of roughly where we are.[18] You can never know if the market is going higher or lower in the short term, but having some idea of whether this is a time where you should be more aggressive or more conservative may pay off. If you are a stock picker, however, you will generally be better off deploying your capital into undervalued stocks not trying to time the market. Given the cyclical nature of most industries, and trends within types of stocks and market sectors, it is rare to find a time that the overall market valuation provides no scope for investment opportunities. Even in 1999, when the overall market hit valuation levels that were the highest ever and was widely considered over-valued, savvy value investors were picking up ignored old-economy quality companies at single digit price-earnings ratios. Those investors generated great returns over the following years, despite the general market weakness.

So, in summary, deciding how to weight the stocks in your portfolio is vitally important to your success as an investor. Most of the well-known simple ways to approach portfolio weighting have some significant drawbacks, and the complex ones have significant barriers to implementation. I have presented a way that is both simple to understand, is based on sound logic and uses proven mathematical theory. Like all aspects of this book, the biggest challenge will not be in understanding but in implementation. Given your unique investment strategy, how you work out these principles in your portfolio may vary. One thing is certain though, time spent building these principles into your portfolio is at least as valuable as the time you will spend finding your next great stock.

12
Maintaining an Optimal Portfolio

No plan survives contact with the enemy[1]

Helmuth von Moltke

By now you should have created an optimal portfolio based on a strategy that is aligned to your competitive advantages and your unique personality and skills, as well as being weighted according to your assessment of the potential upside and downside risk of each holding. Portfolios evolve over time, though: capital is added or removed, and holdings will be subject to a continual stream of price movements due to news, results, market conditions or simply noise. The challenge now is to maintain your optimal portfolio.

You may buy a small high-risk position that goes up significantly and becomes a large position. This then has increased downside risk but reduced upside. Its valuation may have even become stretched yet it has become one of your biggest positions. Logic says that your portfolio is no longer optimal, but taking action always has a cost associated with it, emotionally as well as monetarily. The process of maintaining any dynamic portfolio has to consider the opposing forces of the benefit of rebalancing and the cost of doing so. In the short term we tend to regret errors of commission, the stocks that we sold that kept going up, more than errors of omission, the stock that we failed to sell that carried on going down. Buying or selling a stock will incur a broker commission, may give rise to a tax liability, and there will always be a spread between the price that you can buy and sell stocks at. This means that rebalancing your portfolio too often will expose you to regret, drive unnecessary costs, and reduce returns. Not rebalancing often enough will lead to sub-optimal weightings, with a subsequent lowering of your return profile.

The answer to this conundrum is to mimic the way that control systems, such as thermostats, prevent overly frequent switching: implement a higher threshold to re-balance rather than to retain the status quo. Instead of acting as soon as your portfolio weighting differs from your target percentage, you would act when the weighting differs by plus or minus an additional amount. Say, for example, you have a stock with a target weighting of 5% in your portfolio (based on your estimate of its upside potential and downside risk) and you decide on a rebalancing threshold of 50%. This would mean if the stock rose to become greater than 7.5% (the 5% target weighting multiplied by 100% plus the additional 50% threshold) of your portfolio you would sell some to bring it back to approximately the 5% weighting (assuming the risk-reward estimates have not been sufficiently altered by the 50% rise in the share price). Conversely, if the portfolio weighting of the stock fell below 2.5% (the 5% target weighting multiplied by 100% minus the additional 50% threshold) then you would add to the position to bring it up to the 5% portfolio weighting, (assuming you had the cash to do so and adding to the position didn't violate your rules on limiting your at-cost position size).

One of the common concerns with using this rebalancing process is that it may go against the idea of cutting your losers and running your winners. Running your winners is generally good advice since share prices exhibit medium-term momentum as the market often initially under-reacts to good news. If momentum is a factor that you use to determine the potential upside of a stock, then increased momentum would increase the potential upside and would increase your target weighting. In this case, rebalancing may not be necessary, but you should always this a conscious decision; as I mentioned in the previous chapter, hedge fund managers' largest positions tend to be their worst performers, indicating they often run their winners too far. The other thing to remember about choosing to rebalance is that you are adjusting the weighting of a holding, not selling out completely. You can still run your winners but in a position size that more accurately reflects the right balance between your current assessment of risk and reward.

Cutting your losers can also be good advice, due to the momentum effect and because loss aversion can cause poor decision-making. Ways to mitigate the impact of behavioural biases are covered in Part Two and include using stop-losses if they fit with your strategy. In this case, you may prefer to sell a losing investment rather than adding to it to bring it up to target weight. Typically, the stop loss thresholds that investors choose to use are smaller than the size of the thresholds that would make sense to choose for re-balancing. In this case, a position would never reach the level where you would add to an underweight position, removing this dilemma.

If you are still not convinced that reducing the position size of a winning investment is a good idea, you may want to employ a version of the *trailing stop-loss* discussed in Chapter 8, 'Overcoming Loss Aversion'. Recall that this is where you move your stop-loss to a higher level as the share price of your successful investment goes up. In this case, you allow your portfolio weighting to go above your threshold for rebalancing positions but only while the share price continues to climb. As soon as the price momentum fades, however, and the share price drops below your trailing stop you should significantly reduce the position back to target weighting, or sell out completely if the risk-reward ratio is no longer favourable. This can be a highly effective way of capturing a significant proportion of the upside of a share price movement but is psychologically hard to do since selling at a price lower than the recent peak share price is likely to create strong feelings of regret in most people. If you utilise this strategy you have to be willing to strictly follow your rule to reduce or sell on any drop below the trailing stop. If you are unable to do this consistently, you may be better off following a rebalancing strategy that ignores share price momentum.

One final note of caution with this strategy: your absolute upper portfolio limit should remain in place even for stocks with share price momentum and a trailing stop-loss. Recall that this limit is a mitigation for the impact that unknown unknowns will have on your portfolio. If a company suffers from accounting fraud or some similar significant unexpected negative development, you are unlikely to be able to sell at the value you have set your trailing stop-loss at. In extreme cases, stocks can be suspended from the market and you may not be able to sell at all. The recent demise of Patisserie Valerie is a case in point; a trailing stop is unlikely to have saved investors in this company from a total loss following its suspension and failure.

Utilising a rebalancing methodology that reduces a position when it becomes too large and adds to it when it becomes too small, with thresholds where you take no action, also accounts for the inherent uncertainty in your assessments of upside potential and risk. In reality, you don't have a precise figure for the ideal portfolio weighting but an approximation. Therefore, you want to set sufficiently wide thresholds to take account of the uncertainty in your estimates.

Although you may apply absolute thresholds, that is rebalancing at a target weighting plus or minus a set percentage of your total portfolio, I personally prefer relative ones like the example above. It makes sense to me that I should trim an ideally 2% holding at 3% and an ideally 5% holding at 7.5% rather than 6%.

Finally, there are a couple of additional behavioural biases to be aware of that particularly affect the portfolio rebalancing process, and of course, you will want to try to avoid these in your decision-making process.

Ownership Bias

Ownership Bias, also known as the *Endowment Effect*, is where we tend to overvalue the items we own compared with equivalent items that we don't own. There is a widely replicated experiment that demonstrates how pervasive ownership bias is.[2] At the start of the experiment, participants are randomly allocated items of equal value, such as a mug or a chocolate bar. On average, prior to being allocated the items the participants typically indicate no real preference for one item over the other. After they are allocated the items they are allowed to swap them with fellow participants to obtain their preferred item, or in some versions of the experiment exchange the item for a monetary sum. Given that some participants would have preferred to have received the alternative item from the one they were allocated, you would expect that about half the participants would choose to swap their items. In reality, almost no-one ends up swapping. The reason for the lack of swaps is revealed when participants are asked to assign monetary values to the items. Those who have been given the chocolate bar value the chocolate bar more than 25% higher than those who haven't.[3] The same effect occurs with those who have been given the mug. Ownership bias causes almost no overlap between the value ranges of each item for those who own the item and those who don't own it. When you take into account these value ranges, it is no surprise that no swaps took place. What is surprising is that the only thing that created the difference was which item the participants had been randomly given.

Ownership bias means that you are more likely to overvalue the stocks that you own compared with those that you don't currently own. You are less likely to sell stocks that no longer meet your investment criteria than you would be without suffering from ownership bias.

The only way to overcome this is to periodically plan your ideal portfolio as if you were building a portfolio from scratch and compare it with your current portfolio. Although hard to do, this thought experiment is worth persevering with. Start by listing all stocks that you currently have on your watchlist, or run a screen for stocks that meet your investment criteria. Then run through your list with your checks to eliminate stocks at risk of being frauds, fads or failures. Then assess how risky you believe each stock to be and how much upside potential it has. This will allow you to allocate an ideal portfolio weight to each stock. Take the list of all stocks that have a non-zero weighting and then add up the total weighting of all proposed holdings. If this comes to more than 100% then scale back your ideal weightings to that level. This gives you your ideal portfolio if you were to start investing with a lump sum today with no prior holdings.

By comparing this ideal portfolio to your current portfolio, you should highlight any inconsistencies in your current thinking. If you own stocks in your actual portfolio that you don't allocate any capital to in your ideal portfolio, this may represent ownership bias and is an indication that you should probably sell those stocks and re-invest elsewhere.

Anchoring

Another common bias that impacts investment decisions is *anchoring*. It seems that we are really bad at making absolute judgements. We are subconsciously influenced by the initial values we encounter, even when we know these values are arbitrary. It is the reason the half-price sale is so effective for clothes retailers; we compare the items with their original price rather than the price of similar items in other stores.

Our tendency to become anchored on initial figures has been demonstrated by numerous academic studies over the years. Most of them follow a relatively simple process. First, they expose study participants to a random number by asking them to write down the last three digits of their social security number, bank account number or student number. They then ask them to estimate a series of unknown facts, for example, the population of Denver. The strange thing is that when the researchers compare the answers given to the questions they often correlate with the random number written down first: subjects whose social security number happens to end in a low number tend to provide lower answers for their population estimates than those whose social security number ends in a large number. Of course, this effect is entirely subconscious; no subject thinks that their social security number has any bearing on the population of Denver but being exposed to it does have an impact on their estimate, it seems.

Since investors are exposed to arbitrary numbers all the time, investing is a pursuit where anchoring can be particularly pervasive. We look at charts of share prices and think that, if a stock was trading at £2 per share, it must be cheap at £1 per share, because we subconsciously compare it with previous trading prices. Unless you are an investor whose methodology relies on the signal of price charts to make investment decisions, you may be better off ignoring price charts in your decision-making process to limit the anchoring effect. The temptation to anchor on previous prices is both powerful and subconscious, making it particularly challenging to overcome in our decision-making process.

A value that we can become particularly fixated on, despite it being entirely arbitrary, is our buy price for an individual stock. Hersh Shefrin calls one common investor behaviour, that is caused by anchoring on purchase prices, *get-even-itis*.[4] You may have suffered from this during your investment career. If you have ever found yourself saying 'I'm getting out of this stock as soon as I get my money back' you probably had an acute case. It starts when you have a position that goes against you. As it appears *red* in your portfolio you begin to worry. As it drops further you think 'I wish I'd sold when I first started to worry'. The worry starts to subside as it starts to bottom out and is replaced with a sense of relief as it begins to rise. Then, as soon as it gets back to your buy price, you are so relieved you immediately sell. You probably even pat yourself on the back for getting out without taking a loss. There's that loss aversion popping up again. If nothing has changed since you bought, then the share price going down and up again has not changed the investment case. Equally, if the investment case has deteriorated, you should have sold immediately and it is merely luck that enabled you to sell out at break-even. Given the power of this effect, it may be worth setting a rule that you will never sell a share at your buy price, particularly when the share price trajectory has been a drop and recovery on no news.

A more advanced version of this rule is to try to forget your buy price completely. This is easier said than done, though, because it is often etched in our memory and displayed prominently in our brokerage accounts. The way I try to avoid anchoring is by checking the status of my investments via a spreadsheet that contains live pricing but doesn't contain any record of my buy price. I still have access to this information if I need it for tax purposes or similar valid reasons, but the day-to-day investment process is focussed purely on how individual stock positions match up to my ideal weight for them. I find hiding my buy price often stops me making poor investment decisions, such as adding to a share simply because it is my biggest loser or failing to sell a position because doing so would involve taking a loss.

Tax Effects

One of the reasons many people are slow to rebalance their portfolio is to avoid or delay paying taxes on the profits from selling profitable positions. I am fortunate that, as a UK resident, I have been able to build a portfolio almost entirely in tax-sheltered accounts. There was a time when smaller UK companies listed on the Alternative Investment Market (AIM) were not allowed in tax-sheltered accounts and at this time I had a position that had considerable gains. Since I had used up my capital gains tax-free allowance for that year, I delayed rebalancing my portfolio until the next tax year. By the time the next tax year had come around the position had dropped by more than the tax that would have been due. This is, of course, just a single anecdote; however, the old adage 'don't let the tax tail wag the investment dog' has much validity here. The key is to consider the tax effect as a part of a holistic view of rebalancing. If you have a higher upside or lower risk opportunity, even after selling and paying the tax, then you should sell and redeploy your capital. If you don't have a better opportunity but think the future returns of the stock will be negative, you should also sell and pay the tax. Ownership bias usually leads you to over-value what you own, so if you think the outlook for a stock you own is poor, it probably is worse in reality than the cost of any tax you would have to pay.

Once you have a good understanding of what constitutes an optimal portfolio for you, it is possible to maintain it. The key to dealing with the inherent uncertainty is to err on the side of inaction, just not too much. Using rebalancing thresholds allows exactly that. Like all of the rules in this book, though, it will be a lot easier to define than stick to. Having used this portfolio management strategy successfully for a number of years, then I can guarantee that you will face some challenges using it to rebalance your portfolio. The most common temptation I find is to redefine my risk and reward categorisations to justify a larger position size as a stock increases in value. Almost without exception, when I've done this it has been a mistake. Again, we return to the studies of expert judgement that suggest that when experts use their personal judgment to overrule a well-thought-out rules-based strategy it produces a worse outcome. By understanding this, and how other behavioural biases are likely to lead us astray, you should be better equipped to implement the necessary portfolio rebalancing when it becomes necessary.

Conclusion

> Investing is simple but not easy.
>
> Warren Buffett

The key to excellent investing is doing the simple but difficult consistently well. It is simple to understand that you need to invest where you have an edge but much harder to identify and stick to the sources of edge you possess. It is simple to read about behavioural biases and identify them in others, much harder to see them in your own behaviour and modify it in real-time. It is simple to create a series of portfolio rules to mitigate the impact of your behavioural biases, much harder to follow them. It is simple to think about the risk and reward of individual stocks when determining an ideal position size, much harder to take action to make sure your portfolio remains optimal. Being able to do all of these requires considered thought and discipline.

Following the example of Atul Gawande in *The Checklist Manifesto*, you should seriously consider creating an investment checklist to help you maintain your investment discipline; in fact, create two checklists.

The first checklist will be to help you assess individual stocks. The questions will vary significantly depending on what type of investor you are, but one question that should be on everyone's checklist is *'why* is this mispriced?' If you can't identify why the market may be mispricing the stock and why you can take advantage of the mispricing but others can't, then you should be very wary of investing. In this checklist will be the rules that you use to try to avoid frauds, fads and failures. You should also use this to help you to assess the risk and potential return of an individual stock and therefore guide how large your ideal position would be if the stock meets your investment criteria.

The second type of checklist should be for your overall portfolio. Here you should codify your rules on position size, stop-losses and thresholds for portfolio rebalancing. This is the checklist you should use to periodically review your portfolio and make the necessary adjustments to remain optimal over time.

By making written checklists you are harnessing the power of consistency to hold yourself accountable to your investment strategy. You can increase its power by making the commitment public. While sharing your portfolio in an open forum is likely to have significant drawbacks for your ability to change your mind, sharing your *strategy* with a select few will increase your subconscious desire to be consistent to it. Sharing your portfolio rules with your partner, a friend or a trusted advisor will help you obey them.

If you have the skills, then building your portfolio rules into the spreadsheet or similar system you use to track your investments is also a good idea. This acts as both a reminder of the rules you have set and a prompt to obey them. Since live stock pricing is available in a number of spreadsheet programs, such as Google Sheets[1] or Microsoft Excel in Office 365[2], this gives the ability to dynamically check your portfolio against your investment rules in real-time.

By now, I hope I have convinced you of the importance of good portfolio construction and provided you with the tools to enable you to play to your strengths and overcome your weaknesses. We cannot completely avoid making mistakes as investors: the highly competitive nature of markets, combined with the impact of the psychological biases that affect us all, means that even the world's best investors don't get it right all the time. One of the key messages of this book is that it is not enough to just try harder when we make a mistake. Effort alone is not particularly effective at overcoming behavioural biases due to their often-unconscious effect. To be effective, we have to analyse our past mistakes and identify where we can implement strategies that mitigate the impact of those mistakes *ahead* of our future decision-making process. If we can do that successfully, the results of our efforts will be rewarding. The power of compound returns, 'the eighth wonder of the world' as it is sometimes called, means that even satisfactory market-beating results, over the long term, will generate a secure financial future for you and your family.[3] I hope that this book has been a small but significant step on your journey towards that goal

.

Appendix A
The Kelly Formula

In investment scenarios, the Kelly Criterion formula can be written as follows:

$$\text{Optimal Proportion of Portfolio} = \frac{p}{A} - \frac{q}{B}$$

Where:

    p = the probability of success

    q = the probability of failure = $1 - p$

    B = your return if the outcome is successful, i.e. your investment goes from 1 to $1 + B$

    A = your loss if the outcome is a failure, i.e. your investment goes from 1 to $1 - A$

There may be times when you can directly apply this formula to investing opportunities. Say, for example, there is a rumour of a corporate takeover for a particular stock and the share price is currently £1.00 to buy. You assess that if there is a takeover announced the offer is likely to be around £1.50. However, if the rumour turns out not to be true the share price will drop back to 80p. You think there is a 30% chance that there will be a takeover.

In this case, the Kelly Criterion says that it would be optimal to put:

$$\frac{0.3}{0.2} - \frac{0.7}{0.5} = 0.1$$

Or 10% of your portfolio in this.

In reality, it would be wise to under-bet compared with the Kelly proportion to account for the possibility of being overconfident in the assessment of these probabilities.

It is worth noting that, if you have investment opportunities where you cannot lose more than a small proportion of your investment, and therefore A is small, the Kelly formula may suggest that you bet more than 100% of your portfolio. This implies that you would gear up your investment to maximise your return. In *extremis*, if you had an investment with a positive expectation and no downside at all, the Kelly proportion would be infinite; it would be logical to borrow as much as much money as you possibly could to invest. In reality, of course, every investment has a set of events so extreme that they would cause a total loss. Therefore, gearing up individual investments to multiples of your portfolio value is unlikely to be a good strategy. If B is zero, you get a negatively infinite proportion, indicating that it would be illogical to invest where you have zero upside in your investment.

With these constraints, the number of opportunities to directly apply the Kelly formula to your investments is likely to be quite limited, but that does not mean that the formula has no value: it is by looking at the variables that form the Kelly formula that we derive the principles of portfolio management contained in Chapter 11: As p, the probability of a successful investment outcome, increases, p divided by A increases, and q divided by B decreases, so the optimal proportion of the portfolio to allocate to that investment increases. Likewise, as B, the upside return increases, q divided by B decreases, so the optimal proportion of the portfolio to allocate to that investment increases. Conversely, as A, the downside risk, increases, p divided by A decreases, so the optimal proportion of the portfolio to allocate to that investment decreases.

Appendix B
Bayes Formula

Bayes formula is usually given in the following form:

$$P(A|B) = \frac{P(B|A)\,P(A)}{P(B)}$$

Where:

$P(A|B)$ is the probability of A occurring if B is true.

$P(B|A)$ is the probability of B occurring if A is true.

$P(A)$ and $P(B)$ are the probabilities of A and B occurring independently of each other.

$P(A)$ can also be thought of as the base rate.

In the example in Chapter 7, you read an article in a newspaper reporting a takeover rumour of a certain company and want to know the chance of a successful takeover in the next year *given* that there has been a rumour in the newspaper.

2% of companies receive a takeover in any given year, 5% have rumours in newspapers, and out of the companies that receive a takeover historically, 50% first had a rumour in the newspaper. You want to know how likely is it that your holding will receive a takeover *given* that there is a rumour in the press.

Bayes Theorem says that:

$$P(\text{Takeover}|\text{Rumour}) = \frac{P(\text{Rumour}|\text{Takeover})\, P(\text{Takeover})}{P(\text{Rumour})}$$

$$P(\text{Takeover}|\text{Rumour}) = \frac{0.5 \times 0.02}{0.05} = 0.2$$

Or, 20% chance of a takeover.

Notes and References

Introduction

1. Brad M. Barber and Terrance Odean, *The Behavior of Individual Investors*, September 7, 2011.

https://papers.ssrn.com/sol3/papers.cfm?abstract_id=1872211
or http://dx.doi.org/10.2139/ssrn.1872211

2. Elroy Dimson, Paul Marsh and Mike Staunton, *Credit Suisse Global Investment Returns Yearbook 2018*, Credit Suisse Research Institute, 2018.

https://www.credit-suisse.com/media/assets/corporate/docs/about-us/media/media-release/2018/02/giry-summary-2018.pdf

3. Warren E. Buffett, *1987 Berkshire Hathaway Inc. Annual Shareholder Letter*, 29 February 1988.

4. Daniel Kahneman, quoted in 'How to lean against your biases: A conversation with Daniel Kahneman', *American Press Institute*, June 2014.

https://www.americanpressinstitute.org/publications/good-questions/lean-biases-conversation-daniel-kahneman/

Chapter 1 - Competitive Advantage

1. Michael J. Mauboussin, *Death, Taxes, and Reversion to the Mean*, Legg Mason Capital Management, 14 December 2007.

2. Eugene F. Fama and Kenneth R. French, *Common risk factors in the returns on stocks and bonds*, Journal of Financial Economics, vol. 33, 1993, pp. 3-56.

http://citeseerx.ist.psu.edu/viewdoc/summary?doi=10.1.1.139.5892

3. Jesse Livermore (Psuedonym), Chris Meredith and Patrick O'Shaughnessy, *Factors from Scratch: A look back, and forward, at how, when, and why factors work*, May 2018.

https://www.osam.com/Commentary/factors-from-scratch

4. Warren Buffett and Carol Loomis, 'Mr. Buffett on the Stock Market The most celebrated of investors says stocks can't possibly meet the public's expectations', *Fortune Magazine*, 22 November, 1999.

https://archive.fortune.com/magazines/fortune/fortune_archive/1999/11/22/269071/index.htm

5. https://www.stockopedia.com/, accessed 5 January 2019.

6. As reported by Jeff D. Opdyke and Jane J. Kim, 'Winning Stock Picker's Losing Fund', *The Wall Street Journal*, 16 September, 2004.

https://www.wsj.com/articles/SB109528693813819017

7. Joel Greenblatt, *The Little Book that Beats the Market*, John Wiley & Sons, 2005.

8. Wesley R. Gray and Tobias E. Carlisle, *Quantitative Value*, John Wiley & Sons, 2013.

9. Joel Greenblatt, 'Adding Your Two Cents May Cost a Lot Over the Long Term', *Joel Greenblatt's Perspectives*, Morningstar, 18 January 2012.

http://socialize.morningstar.com/NewSocialize/blogs/joelgreenblatt/archive/2012/01/18/adding-your-two-cents-may-cost-a-lot-over-the-long-term.aspx

10. Frederik Vanhaverbeke, *Excess Returns*, Harriman House, 2014. Table 1.

Chapter 2 - Think Small

1. Based on The Investment Association estimate of £1.2 trillion UK investment funds' Assets Under Management in 2018 and approximately 2,500 UK investment funds from the *2014-5 Investment Association Annual Survey* and author's calculations.

https://www.theinvestmentassociation.org/

2. https://www.stockopedia.com/, accessed on 23 December 2018.

3. Russell Kinnel, 'What's the Right Size for Your Fund?', *Morningstar FundInvestor*, August 2017 as quoted in Richard Loth, 'Fund Size and Performance', *investopedia.com*, undated.

https://www.morningstar.com/articles/826450/whats-the-right-size-for-your-fund.html

https://www.investopedia.com/university/quality-mutual-fund/chp5-fund-size/

4. Investment Company Institute, *2018 Investment Company Fact Book*, Table 2, and author's calculations.

5. Warren E. Buffett, *Partnership Letter*, Buffett Partnership Limited, 29 May 1969. As quoted by Jeremy Miller, *Warren Buffett's Ground Rules*, Profile Books, 2016, p. 258.

6. Lars Kroijer, *Money Mavericks: Confessions of a Hedge Fund Manager*, Pearson Education Limited, 2010, p. 65.

7. Larry Swedroe, 'Passive Investing Misconceptions', from Meb Faber (ed.), *The Best Investment Writing Volume 2*, Harriman House, 2018, p. 186. Originally published 5 September 2017.

https://www.etf.com/sections/index-investor-corner/swedroe-passive-investing-misconceptions/

8. Directive 2014/65/EU of the European Parliament and of the Council of 15 May 2014 on markets in financial instruments and amending Directive 2002/92/EC and Directive 2011/61/EU (recast).

https://www.esma.europa.eu/policy-rules/mifid-ii-and-mifir

9. Elroy Dimson, Paul Marsh, Mike Staunton, *Credit Suisse Global Investment Returns Yearbook 2018*, Credit Suisse Research Institute, 2018.

https://www.credit-suisse.com/media/assets/corporate/docs/about-us/media/media-release/2018/02/giry-summary-2018.pdf

10. *Kenneth R. French – Data Library* and author's calculations.

https://mba.tuck.dartmouth.edu/pages/faculty/ken.french/data_library.html

11. Cliff S. Asness, et al., *Size Matters, If You Control Your Junk*, Fama-Miller Working Paper, 22 January 2015.

SSRN: https://ssrn.com/abstract=2553889 or http://dx.doi.org/10.2139/ssrn.2553889

12. Ibid.

13. Ibid.

14. Eugene F. Fama and Kenneth R. French quoted in Schultz Collins Lawson Chambers Inc., *Update on the Value Premium*, May, 2014.

http://schultzcollins.com/static/uploads/2016/08/Update-on-the-Value-Premium.pdf

15. Ibid.

16. Ibid.

17. Ludovic Phalippou, *What Drives The Value Premium?*, 2004.

https://www.semanticscholar.org/paper/What-Drives-The-Value-Premium-%3F-Phalippou/515d1f3579a94bde641a554a105904d8b4ea544d

Chapter 3 - Think Long Term

1. John Robert Graham, Campbell R. Harvey and Shivaram Rajgopal, *The Economic Implications of Corporate Financial Reporting*, 11 January 2005.

SSRN: https://ssrn.com/abstract=491627 or http://dx.doi.org/10.2139/ssrn.491627

2. Warren E. Buffett, *Partnership Letter*, Buffett Partnership Limited, 29 May 1969. As quoted by Jeremy Miller in *Warren Buffett's Ground Rules*, Profile Books, 201, p. 258.

3. James Mackintosh, 'The fatal effect of the 'career risk' fear', *Financial Times*, 13 May 2012.

4. State Street Global Advisors, *Building Bridges*, 2015.

5. Adam McKay, Ryan Gosling, Christian Bale, Brad Pitt and Steve Carell. 2016. *The big short*.

Michael Lewis, *The Big Short*, Penguin Books, 2011.

6. https://en.wikipedia.org/wiki/Michael_Burry, accessed 23 December 2018.

7. David Dremen, *Contrarian Investment Strategies*, FREE PRESS, 1998, pp. 160-169.

8. Meb Faber, 'The Dividend Growth Myth', *mebfaber.com* [blog], 26 April 2017.

https://mebfaber.com/2017/04/26/dividend-growth-myth/

NOTES AND REFERENCES

Chapter 4 - Think Differently

1. Antti Ilmanen, *Expected Returns: An Investor's Guide to Harvesting Market Rewards*, John Wiley & Sons, 2011, p. 184-185.

2. Ibid, p184.

3. Patrick J. Cusatis, James A. Miles and J. Randall Woolridge, *Restructuring Through Spinoffs*, Journal of Financial Economics, 33, 1993.

4. Joel Greenblatt, *You Can Be a Stock Market Genius: Uncover the Secret Hiding Places of Stock Market Profits*, Fireside, 1999.

Chapter 5 - Know Yourself

1. Kent D. Daniel, *Momentum Crashes*, Columbia Business School Research Paper No. 11-03, 12 April, 2011.

SSRN: https://ssrn.com/abstract=1914673 or http://dx.doi.org/10.2139/ssrn.1914673

2. Cliff S. Asness, 'Liquid Alt Ragnarök?', *Cliff's Perspective* [blog], AQR Capital Management, 7 September 2018.

https://www.aqr.com/Insights/Perspectives/Liquid-Alt-Ragnarok

3. Wesley R. Gray, 'Even God Would Get Fired as an Active Investor', *Alpha Architect* [blog], 2 February 2016.

https://alphaarchitect.com/2016/02/02/even-god-would-get-fired-as-an-active-investor/

4. Angela L. Duckworth, et al., *Grit: Perseverance and passion for long-term goals*, Journal of Personality and Social Psychology, vol. 92, no. 6, June 2007, pp. 1087–1101.

https://www.researchgate.net/publication/6290064_Grit_Perseverance_and_Passion_for_Long-Term_Goals

5. Ibid.

6. Ibid.

7. Carol S. Dweck, *Mindset: How You Can Fulfil Your Potential*, Robinson, 2012.

8. Rolf Dobelli, *The Art of the Good Life: Clear Thinking for Business and a Better Life*, Hodder & Stoughton Ltd, 2017, p. 210.

9. Henrik Cronqvist, Stephan Siegel and Frank Yu, *Value versus growth investing: Why do different investors have different styles?*, Journal of Financial Economics, vol. 117, no. 2, August 2015, pp. 333-349.

https://ssrn.com/abstract=2351123 or http://dx.doi.org/10.2139/ssrn.2351123

10. Thomas J. Bouchard Jr., et al., *Sources of Human Psychological Differences: The Minnesota Study of Twins Reared Apart*, Science, vol. 250, no. 4978, 12 October 1990, pp. 223-228. DOI: 10.1126/science.2218526

11. Cronqvist.

12. Elke U. Weber, Ann-Rene E. Blais and Nancy E. Betz, *Domain-specific Risk-attitude Scale: Measuring Risk Perceptions and Risk Behaviors*, Journal of Behavioral Decision Making, vol. 15, 2002, pp. 263–290. DOI: 10.1002/bdm.414

13. Cliff S. Asness, 'Our Model Goes to Six and Saves Value from Redundancy Along the Way', *Cliff's Perspective* [blog], AQR Capital Management, 17 December 2014.

https://www.aqr.com/Insights/Perspectives/Our-Model-Goes-to-Six-and-Saves-Value-From-Redundancy-Along-the-Way

14. Cara Scatizzi, 'Finding Value Among the "Lows": The Walter J. Schloss Approach', *Journal of American Association of Individual Investors*, October 2009.

https://www.aaii.com/journal/article/finding-value-amoung-the-lows-the-walter-j-schloss-approach

15. John M. Digman, *Personality Structure: Emergence of the Five-Factor Model*, Annual Review of Psychology, 1990, p417-440.

16. Malcolm Gladwell, 'Malcolm Gladwell's 12 Rules for Life', *Revisionist History* [Podcast], Season 3, Episode 7.

http://revisionisthistory.com/episodes/27-malcolm-gladwell-s-12-rules-for-life

17. Bruce N. Lehmann, *Fads, Martingales, and Market Efficiency*, The Quarterly Journal of Economics, vol. 105, no. 1, 1 February 1990, pp. 1–28.

https://doi.org/10.2307/2937816

18. Xin Hong, Bradford D. Jordan and Mark H. Liu, *Industry Information and the 52-Week High Effect*, 15 October 2011.

https://ssrn.com/abstract=1787378 or http://dx.doi.org/10.2139/ssrn.1787378

19. John M. Griffin, Susan Ji and J. Spencer Martin, *Global Momentum Strategies: A Portfolio Perspective*, 15 July 2004.

https://ssrn.com/abstract=492804 or http://dx.doi.org/10.2139/ssrn.492804

20. From 'Momentum Effect in Stocks', *quantpedia.com* based on data from *Kenneth R. French – Data Library*.

https://quantpedia.com/screener/Details/14

http://mba.tuck.dartmouth.edu/pages/faculty/ken.french/data_library.html

21. Gary Antonacci, 'Mistakes of Momentum Investors', *Dual Momentum Blog* [blog], 30 November 2016.

https://www.dualmomentum.net/2016/11/common-mistakes-of-momentum-investors_30.html

22. https://en.wikipedia.org/wiki/Gerald_Ratner, accessed 6 February 2019.

23. Christopher Mayer, *100 baggers*, Laissez Faire Books, 2015.

24. Peter Lynch, *One Up on Wall Street*, Simon & Schuster, 2000.

25. Jim Slater, *The Zulu Principle: Making Extraordinary Profits from Ordinary Shares*, Texere, 1997.

26. Cronqvist.

27. Walter J. Schloss, *Columbia Business School Upper Level Seminar in Value Investing* [Lecture], 17 November 1993.

http://csinvesting.org/wp-content/uploads/2014/10/schloss_lecture.pdf

28. Edwin Lefevre, *Reminiscences of a Stock Operator*, John Wiley & Sons, Inc., 1994, p. 154.

29. Peter Lynch, *One Up on Wall Street*, Simon & Schuster, 2000.

30. Warren E. Buffett, *1988 Berkshire Hathaway Inc. Annual Shareholder Letter*, 28 February 1989.

31. Lee Freeman-Shor, *The Art of Execution*, Harriman House, 2015.

32. John Hempton, 'When do you average down?', *Bronte Capital Blog*, 4 January 2017.

http://brontecapital.blogspot.com/2017/01/when-do-you-average-down.html

33. Wall Street Physician [Pseudonym], 'Wall Street Profiles: Bill Miller, Legg Mason Value Trust', *Wall Street Physician*[website], 23 August 2017.

https://www.wallstreetphysician.com/wall-street-profiles-bill-miller-legg-mason-value-trust/

34. Ibid.

Chapter 6 - Behavioural Biases

1. Antonio R. Damasio, *Descartes' Error: Emotion, Reason, and the Human Brain*, Avon Books, 1994, pp. 193-194.

2. Amos Tverky would undoubtedly have shared Kahneman's 2002 Nobel Prize had he not died in 1996.

3. Robert B. Cialdini, *Influence: The Psychology of Persuasion*, HarperCollins, 1 February 2007, pp. 87-125.

4. Daniel Kahneman, *Thinking, Fast and Slow*, Penguin Books, 2011.

5. Ibid.

6. E.J. Masicampo and Roy F. Baumeister, *Toward a Physiology of Dual-Process Reasoning and Judgment: Lemonade, Willpower, and Expensive Rule-Based Analysis*, 1 March 2008.

https://doi.org/10.1111/j.1467-9280.2008.02077.x

7. John Medina, *Brain Rules*, Pear Press, 2014, p. 47.

8. David F. Dinges, et al., *Cumulative Sleepiness, Mood Disturbance, and Psychomotor Vigilance Performance Decrements During a Week of Sleep Restricted to 4-5 Hours Per Night*, Sleep 20, 1997, pp. 267-277.

9. https://en.wikipedia.org/wiki/Dunning%E2%80%93Kruger_effect, accessed on 20 March 2019.

10. Kenneth Abernathy, et al., *Alcohol and the prefrontal cortex*, International review of neurobiology, vol. 91, 2010, pp. 289-320.

11. **"Predictably Irrational"**. This is the title of a great book on the topic by behavioural economist Dan Ariely.

12. Atul Gawande, *The Checklist Manifesto*, Profile Books, 2011.

13. http://www.who.int/patientsafety/topics/safe-surgery/checklist/en/

14. Gawande.

15. Michael Lewis, *The Undoing Project*, Penguin Books 2016, pp. 171-173.

Chapter 7 - Overcoming Overconfidence

1. Iain A. McCormick, Frank H. Walkey, Dianne E. Green, *Comparative Perceptions of Driver Ability: A Confirmation and Expansion*, Accident Analysis & Prevention, vol. 18, no. 3, June 1986, pp. 205–208.

2. https://en.wikipedia.org/wiki/French_invasion_of_Russia, accessed on 11 February 2019.

3. https://en.wikipedia.org/wiki/Battle_of_the_Little_Bighorn, accessed on 11 February 2019.

4. Steve Twomey, 'How (Almost) Everyone Failed to Prepare for Pearl Harbor', *Smithsonian Magazine*, December 2016.

https://www.smithsonianmag.com/history/how-almost-everyone-failed-prepare-pearl-harbor-1-180961144/

5. https://en.wikipedia.org/wiki/Battle_of_Midway, accessed on 11 February 2019.

6. Stuart Oskamp, *Overconfidence in case-study judgments*, Journal of Consulting Psychology, vol. 29, no. 3, 1965, pp. 261-265.

7. Nassim Nicholas Taleb, *The Black Swan: The Impact of the Highly Improbable*, Penguin Books, 2007, pp. 129-130.

8. Wrongly attributed to Mark Twain, but probably an adaptation of Josh Billings' writing. See Garson O'Toole, *Quote Investigator* [website].

https://quoteinvestigator.com/2015/05/30/better-know/

9. Warren E. Buffett, *Berkshire Hathaway Annual Shareholder Letter*, 1993.

http://www.berkshirehathaway.com/letters/1993.html

10. Jeremy Miller, *Warren Buffett's Ground Rules*, Profile Books, 2016, pp. 144-145.

11. Andrew Kilpatrick, *Of Permanent Value*, 1996. As quoted in Jeremy Miller, *Warren Buffett's Ground Rules*, Profile Books, 2016, pp. 164-165.

12. Lawrence Fisher and James H Lorie, *Some Studies of Variability of Returns on Investments in Common Stocks*, The Journal of Business, vol. 43, no. 2, 1970, pp. 99-134.

13. Ronald J Surz and Mitchell Price, *The Truth About Diversification by the Numbers*, The Journal of Investing, vol. 9, 2000, pp. 93-95. 10.3905/joi.2000.319444.

14. See, William Poundstone, *Fortunes Formula: The Untold Story of the Scientific Betting System that Beat the Casinos and Wall Street*, Hill and Wang, 2006, for a full history.

15. Nathan Bomey, 'BP's Deepwater Horizon costs total $62B', *USA Today*, 14 July 2016.

https://eu.usatoday.com/story/money/2016/07/14/bp-deepwater-horizon-costs/87087056/

16. Warren E. Buffett, 'The Superinvestors of Graham-and-Doddsville', *Hermes: the Columbia Business School Magazine*, 1984, pp. 4–15.

https://www8.gsb.columbia.edu/sites/valueinvesting/files/files/Buffett1984.pdf

17. Charles Stein, John Gittelsohn and Peggy Collins, 'Goldfarb Exits as Sequoia's Valeant Debacle Caps 45-Year Career', *Bloomberg Business*, 23 March 2016.

18. Thomas Heath, 'An epic winning streak on Wall Street — then one ugly loss', *Washington Post*, 12 August 2017.

https://www.washingtonpost.com/business/capitalbusiness/an-epic-winning-streak-on-wall-street--then-one-ugly-loss/2017/08/11/137fc2dc-7637-11e7-8839-ec48ec4cae25_story.html

19. Philip E. Tetlock and Dan Gardner, *Superforecasting: The Art and Science of Prediction*, Crown Publishing Group, 2015.

20. Daniel Kahneman, *Thinking, Fast and Slow*, Penguin Books, 2011. p. 7.

21. B. J. Carducci and P. G. Zimbardo, *Are you shy?*, Psychology Today, vol. 34–40, no. 64, pp. 66, 68, November/December 1995.

https://people.com/archive/psychologist-philip-zimbardo-leads-shy-people-out-of-the-world-of-wallflowers-vol-7-no-25/

22. Jay R. Ritter, *The Long-Run Performance of Initial Public Offerings*, The Journal of Finance, vol. XLVI, no. 1, March 1991.

https://onlinelibrary.wiley.com/doi/epdf/10.1111/j.1540-6261.1991.tb03743.x

23. Cancer Research UK, Office for National Statistics and author's calculations.

https://www.cancerresearchuk.org/health-professional/cancer-statistics-for-the-uk

https://www.ons.gov.uk/peoplepopulationandcommunity/populationandmigration/populationestimates

Chapter 8 - Overcoming Loss Aversion

1. Daniel Kahneman, *Thinking, Fast and Slow*, Penguin Books, 2011. p. 284.

2. Dan Davies, *Lying for Money*, Profile Books Limited, 2018, pp. 165-173.

3. Hersh Shefrin, *Beyond Greed and Fear: Understanding Behavioural Finance and the Psychology of Investing*, Oxford University Press, 2002, p. 110-115.

Shefrin gives a fuller account of how loss aversion impacted Clinton's decision-making around these events, and how it started much earlier than the Monica Lewinsky affair during his presidency.

4. Lee Freeman-Shor, *The Art of Execution*, Harriman House, 2015.

Chapter 9 - Overcoming Optimism Bias

1. Marianna Masiero, Claudio Lucchiari and Gabriella Pravettoni, *Personal Fable: Optimistic Bias in Cigarette Smokers*, International Journal of High Risk Behaviors & Addiction, vol. 4, no. 1, 1 March 2015. doi: 10.5812/ijhrba.20939.

2. Ed Diener and Micaela Y. Chan, *Happy People Live Longer: Subjective Well-Being Contributes to Health and Longevity*, Applied Psychology: Health and Well-being, vol. 3, no. 1, 2001, pp. 1-43. doi:10.1111/j.1758-0854.2010.01045.x.

3. Robert Bohm et al., *Are we looking for positivity or similarity in a partner's outlook on life? Similarity predicts perceptions of social attractiveness and relationship quality*, Journal of Positive Psychology, vol. 5, no. 6, 2010, pp. 431-438.

4. Longboard Staff, 'Defense Wins Championships: How to build a winning alternatives strategy', *Longboard Funds Insights* [Blog], Undated.

https://www.insights.longboardfunds.com/post/defense-wins-championships

5. David Rocker, *The Short Perspective in Today's Markets*, CFA Institute Conference Proceedings Quarterly, June 2005.

6. Warren E. Buffett, *Berkshire Hathaway Inc. Annual Shareholder Letter*, 23 February 2018, p. 7.

http://www.berkshirehathaway.com/letters/2018ltr.pdf

7. Anthony Bolton, 'Anthony Bolton: Balance sheets are the most common cause of grief', *Financial Times*, 29 February 2008.

8. Paul W. Allen, *Choose Stocks Wisely: A Formula That Produced Amazing Returns*, CreateSpace Independent Publishing Platform, 1 Oct. 2013.

9. Edward I. Altman, *Financial Ratios, Discriminant Analysis and the Prediction of Corporate Bankruptcy*, Journal of Finance, September 1968.

10. Edward I. Altman, *Predicting Financial Distress of Companies: Revisiting the Z-score and Zeta Models*, Handbook of Research Methods and Applications in Empirical Finance, July 2000, pp. 428–456.

11. Robert C. Merton, *On the Pricing of Corporate Debt: The Risk Structure of Interest Rates*, The Journal of Finance, vol. 29, no. 2, May 1974, pp. 449-470.

12. Sreedhar T. Bharath and Tyler Shumway, *Forecasting Default with the Merton Distance to Default Model*, The Review of Financial Studies, vol. 21, no. 3, May 2008, pp. 1339-1369.

13. James A. Ohlson, *Financial Ratios and the Probabilistic Prediction of Bankruptcy*, Journal of Accounting Research, vol. 18, no. 1, Spring 1980, pp. 109-131.

14. John Y Campbell, Jens Dietrich Hilscher and Jan Szilagyi, *Predicting financial distress and the performance of distressed Stocks*, Journal of Investment Management, vol. 9, no. 2, pp. 14-34.

http://nrs.harvard.edu/urn-3:HUL.InstRepos:9887619

15. Joon Ian Wong, 'We finally know how much Nintendo made from Pokémon Go', *Quartz*, 26 October 2016.

https://qz.com/819677/nintendo-pokemon-go-profits-we-finally-know-how-much-nintendo-made-from-pokemon-go/

16. Dan Davies, *Lying for Money*, Profile Books Limited, 2018, p. 11.

17. Financial Reporting Council, *Corporate Reporting Thematic Review: Judgements and Estimates*, November 2017.

https://www.frc.org.uk/getattachment/42301e27-68d8-4676-be4c-0f5605d1b467/091117-Judgements-and-Estimates-CRR-thematic-review.pdf

18. Frank Benford, *The Law of Anomalous Numbers*, Proceedings of the American Philosophical Society, March 1938. Although Simon Newcomb had found the same result as far back as 1881.

19. Messod D. Beneish, *The Detection of Earnings Manipulation*, Financial Analysts Journal, vol. 55, no. 5, September - October 1999, pp. 24-36.

20. UK Financial Reporting Council, *Investigation into the audit of the financial statements of Carillion plc* [Press Release], 29 January 2018.

https://www.frc.org.uk/news/january-2018-(1)/investigation-into-the-audit-of-the-financial-stat

21. UK Financial Reporting Council, *Disciplinary action in relation to Autonomy Corporation plc* [Press Release], 31 May 2018.

https://www.frc.org.uk/news/may-2018/disciplinary-action-in-relation-to-autonomy-corpor

22. Howard M. Schilit, *Financial Shenanigans: How to Detect Accounting Gimmicks & Fraud in Financial Reports*, McGraw-Hill, 2010.

23. Thornton O'Glove, *Quality of Earnings*, Macmillan Inc., 1987.

24. Davies, p. 288.

25. Avner Mandelman, *The Sleuth Investor*, McGraw-Hill, 2007.

26. Davies, pp. 284-285.

27. Davies, pp. 51-63.

28. https://www.investegate.co.uk/globo-plc--gbo-/rns/company-statement/201510260819113872D/

29. All figures in this example are taken from the Historic Regulatory News Statements of the company, accessed on 2 May 2019, from:

https://www.investegate.co.uk/Index.aspx?searchtype=3&words=GBO

30. Veronique Boulenger and Tatjana A. Nazir, *Interwoven Functionality of the Brain's Action and Language Systems*, The Mental Lexicon, vol. 5, no. 2, 2010, pp. 231-254.

31. Nicole K. Speer et al., *Reading Stories Activates Neural Representations of Visual and Motor Experiences*, Psychological Science, vol. 20, no. 8, August 2009, pp. 989–999.

NOTES AND REFERENCES

32. Julio González et al., *Reading cinnamon activates olfactory brain regions*, NeuroImage, vol. 32, no. 2, 15 August 2006, pp. 906-912.

33. Paul J. Zak and Robert Kurzban and William T. Matzner, *Oxytocin is associated with human trustworthiness*, Hormones and Behavior, vol. 48, 2005, pp. 522-527.

http://www.robkurzban.com/articles/2013/10/10/oxytocin-is-associated-with-human-trustworthiness-pdf

34. Rajendra D. Badgaiyan, Alan J. Fischman and Nathaniel M. Alpert, *Dopamine Release During Human Emotional Processing*, Neuroimage, vol. 47, no. 4, 1 October 2009, pp. 2041-2045.

https://www.ncbi.nlm.nih.gov/pmc/articles/PMC2740985/

35. Joshua L. Roffman et al., *Dopamine D1 signaling organizes network dynamics underlying working memory*, Science Advances, vol. 2, no. 6, 3 June 2016.

https://advances.sciencemag.org/content/2/6/e1501672

36. John Maynard Keynes, *General Theory of Employment, Interest And Money*, Macmillan, 1936.

37. This is actually a quote from Irving Kahn's son, Tom Kahn, describing his father's approach, from Richard Evans, '108-year-old investor: 'I doubled my money in 1929 crash – and I'm still winning', *The Telegraph*, 23 August 2014.

https://www.telegraph.co.uk/finance/personalfinance/investing/11048689/108-year-old-investor-I-doubled-my-money-in-1929-crash-and-Im-still-winning.html

38. https://hbr.org/

39. Jim Collins, *Good to Great: Why Some Companies Make the Leap and Others Don't*, Random House Business, 2001.

40. Steven D. Levitt, 'From Good to Great ... to Below Average', *Freakonomics* [blog], 28 July 2008.

http://freakonomics.com/2008/07/28/from-good-to-great-to-below-average/

41. J. Scott Armstrong and Kesten C. Green, *Competitor-oriented objectives: the myth of market share*, International Journal of Business, vol. 12, 2007, pp. 117-136.

https://papers.ssrn.com/sol3/papers.cfm?abstract_id=988441

See Daniel Rasmussen, 'The Gospel According to Michael Porter', *Institutional Investor*, 8 November 2017, for more detail on the topic.

https://www.institutionalinvestor.com/article/b15jm11km848qm/the-gospel-according-to-michael-porter

42. Thomas C. Powell, *Competitive Advantage: Logical and Philosophical* Considerations, Strategic Management Journal, vol. 22, 2001, pp. 875-888. DOI:10.1002/smj.173

43. https://www.investegate.co.uk/patisserie-hldgs-plc--cake-/rns/company-update/201901161553543018N/, accessed on 26 February 2019.

44. Warren E. Buffett, *1999 Berkshire Hathaway Annual Meeting*, as quoted by Mary Buffett and David Clark, *The Tao of Warren Buffett: Warren Buffett's Words of Wisdom*, Simon & Schuster, 2009, p. 145.

Chapter 10 - Overcoming Commitment Bias

1. Robert B. Cialdini, *Influence: The Psychology of Persuasion*, HarperCollins, 2007, p. vii.

2. Ibid, p. 45.

3. Ibid, pp. 55-56.

4. Paul Samuelson questioned by Austin Kiplinger, *Meet The Press*, 20 December 1970. Transcript of the show from *Daily Labor Report*, Bureau of National Affairs, Washington, 21 December 1970.

5. Cialdini, pp. 56-57.

6. Jason Zweig, 'Dinner With Charlie: The World According to Mr. Munger', *Wall Street Journal*, 3 May 2019.

https://www.wsj.com/articles/dinner-with-charlie-the-world-according-to-mr-munger-11556896281

Chapter 11 - Creating an Optimal Portfolio

1. Robert Arnott, Jason Hsu and Phil Moore, *Fundamental Indexation*, Financial Analyst Journal, vol. 61, no. 2, 2005, pp. 83-89.

https://www.researchaffiliates.com/documents/FAJ_Mar_Apr_2005_Fundamental_Indexation.pdf

2. Joe Nocera, 'Passions Run High on Indexing', *New York Times*, 17 May 2008.

https://www.nytimes.com/2008/05/17/business/17nocera.html

3. Robert D Arnott and Lillian J. Wu, *The Winners Curse: Too Big to Succeed?*, Journal of Indexes, 29 October 2012.

https://ssrn.com/abstract=2088515 or http://dx.doi.org/10.2139/ssrn.2088515

4. Meb Faber, *Invest with the House: Hacking the Top Hedge Funds*, The Idea Farm, 2016, p. 152.

https://mebfaber.com/books/

5. Harry M. Markowitz, *Portfolio Selection*, The Journal of Finance, vol. 7, no. 1, March 1952, pp. 77–91. doi:10.2307/2975974. JSTOR 2975974.

6. Antti Ilmanen and Rodney N. Sullivan, *Words From the Wise: Harry Markowitz on Portfolio Theory and Practice*, AQR Capital Management, 29 January 2016.

https://www.aqr.com/Insights/Research/Interviews/Words-From-the-Wise-Harry-Markowitz-on-Portfolio-Theory-and-Practice

7. Edward O. Thorp, *Beat the Dealer*, Random House, 1962.

8. Mohnish Pabrai, *The Dhandho Investor: The Low-Risk Value Method to High Returns*, John Wiley & Sons Inc, New Jersey, 2007.

9. Elroy Dimson, Paul Marsh and Mike Staunton, *Credit Suisse Global Investment Returns Yearbook 2016*, Credit Suisse Research Institute, 2016.

http://investir-et-devenir-libre.com/wp-content/uploads/2017/02/csri-returns-yearbook-2016.pdf

10. William N. Thorndike Jr., *The Outsiders: Eight Unconventional CEOs and Their Radically Rational Blueprint for Success*, Harvard Business Review Press, 2012.

11. Daylian M. Cain, George Loewenstein and Don A. Moore, *The Dirt on Coming Clean: The Perverse Effects of Disclosing Conflicts of Interest*, Journal of Legal Studies, 2005.

12. https://www.transparency.org/research/cpi/overview

13. American Association of Individual Investors, *Asset Allocation Survey*.

Spreadsheet downloaded from https://www.aaii.com/assetallocationsurvey

14. Cullen Roche, 'Why Do Individual Investors Underperform?', *Pragmatic Capitalism Blog*, 22 June 2015.

http://www.pragcap.com/why-do-retail-investors-underperform/

15. Samuel Lee, 'Waiting for the Market to Crash is a Terrible Strategy', from Meb Faber (ed.), *The Best Investment Writing Volume 2*, Harriman House, 2018, p. 229. Originally published 19 May 2017.

https://svrn.co/blog/2017/5/14/waiting-for-the-market-to-crash-is-a-terrible-strategy

16. Russel Kinnel, 'Mind the Gap', from Meb Faber (ed.), *The Best Investment Writing Volume 2*, Harriman House Ltd, Hampshire, 2018, p. 65. Originally published 30 May 2017.

https://www.morningstar.com/articles/810470/mind-the-gap-global-investor-returns-show-the%20cost.html

17. Wesley R. Gray, 'How a Mutual Fund Can Win but Its Investors Still Lose', *The Wall Street Journal*, 7 December 2015.

https://blogs.wsj.com/experts/2015/12/07/how-a-mutual-fund-can-win-but-its-investors-still-lose/

18. Howard Marks, *Mastering the Market Cycle: Getting the Odds on Your Side*, Nicholas Brealey Publishing, 2018.

Chapter 12 - Maintaining an Optimal Portfolio

1. Paraphrased.

2. For example, Daniel Kahneman, Jack L. Knetsch and Richard H Thaler. *Experimental Tests of the Endowment Effect and the Coase Theorem*, Journal of Political Economy, vol. 98, no. 6, 1990, pp. 1325–1348.

3. Jochen Reb and Terry Connolly, *Possession, feelings of ownership and the endowment effect*, Judgment and Decision Making, vol. 2, no. 2, April 2007, pp. 107-114.

4. Hersh Shefrin, *Beyond Greed and Fear: Understanding Behavioural Finance and the Psychology of Investing*, Oxford University Press, 2002, p. 107.

Conclusion

1. https://support.google.com/docs/answer/3093281?hl=en

2. https://support.office.com/en-us/article/get-a-stock-quote-e5af3212-e024-4d4c-bea0-623cf07fbc54

3. This quote is often attributed to Albert Einstein although there appears to be no evidence that he had any view on the topic. See Garson O'Toole, *Quote Investigator* [website].

https://quoteinvestigator.com/2011/10/31/compound-interest/

Printed in Great Britain
by Amazon